COMPUTERS MADE EASY

How To Master Your Computer In Just 2 Hours

Jeff Clarke

How To Master Your Computer in Just 2 Hours
Jeff Clarke

© Copyright MMIII The Windsor Group

Second Edition
Published MMIII by The Windsor Group
The Old School House,
1 St John's Court,
Moulsham Street,
Chelmsford,
Essex CM2 0JD

Typeset by SJ Design and Publishing, Bromley, Kent

ISBN 1-9537074-0-7

Contents

Contents

Part One
Buying a Personal Computer

Chapter 1

Introduction

The world of the personal computer often seems to be a strange one and it can look hostile to outsiders. Jargon, technical detail and mystical abbreviations surround it like a barbed-wire fence. At best, the beginner will feel confused. Unlike games machines and the simple home computers of the early 1980s which made an effort to be friendly, it often seems as if the adepts of personal computing are jealously guarding their secrets, trying to make it hard for others to get involved. If you have ever gone as far as looking at a magazine advert for a personal computer, you will have found that in general it consists of a picture of a box with a screen, and tightly-packed columns of near-gibberish text.

The following 'sales pitch' was all that was given to describe a particular machine in an advert selected at random from a recent popular mainstream computer magazine:

- Intel® Pentium® 4 Processor 1600 MHz

- 256MB RAM

- 40GB Hard Disk Drive

- DVD/CD Re-Writer combined drive

- 17" CRT SVGA Colour Monitor

- (16" Viewable In Screen)

- Microsoft® Windows® XP Home Edition

If you understood anything much out of that mess of jargon then you deserve a hearty pat on the back; you've obviously been doing your homework.

Unfortunately, this sort of product description is standard. It does not help that companies choose to refer to themselves and their products using names that sound like jargon. Only the experienced would be able to tell that the term 'USR' is a company ('*U.S. Robotics*') and that 'KBPS' ('*Thousands of Bits Per Second*') is a technical term, which will be explained later.

This book will tell you what you need to know to be able to decipher the more important parts of computer advertising, and show you how to decide what sort of machine you need and what extras would be useful to you. It would be completely understandable if, faced with the impenetrable description above, you decided that you didn't really need a computer after all. Before we start to look into the world of computers then, we will consider the question of: 'Why bother in the first place?'

The computer revolution

Many of the readers of this book will never have used a computer before, right? Wrong! The *'Computer Revolution'* is not just a flashy media phrase. Computers are now controlling most of our everyday devices. There are too many examples to list more than a tiny fraction of them, but if you use any of the following then you have used a computer:

- washing machines
- pocket calculators
- mobile telephones
- microwave ovens
- auto-bank (ATM) cash dispensers
- video recorders
- certain makes of cars
- certain makes of wristwatches

In that list, the computers are hidden on the inside. In fact, they are all around us in the world and their numbers are increasing all the time.

As the level of technology increases, driven by the never-ending quest for profits, computers will become more and more significant. It is important not to see this as frightening. When you look at it in its simplest form, a computer is just a box that does exactly what it is told to do. While some, like the personal computers that we will be talking about in this book, can do a great many things, others, like those in a washing machine, are extremely limited, and are nothing more than useful tools.

Like any other tool, you need to know what it can do and how to use it before you can get the most from it. Although computers in general have a huge range of uses, and more are being found every day, the personal computer, the box found in many offices and homes, has four main areas of importance. These are in business, communications, leisure and education.

Computers for writers

For many people, business is the primary use for a personal computer. Of all the different work-related tasks that it can help with, the most important is *word processing*. The ability to put text into a computer, edit it, move it around, add **bold emphasis,** *italics* or underlining, and then print it out when it is perfect has helped computers to become an almost standard part of any desk.

Typewriters are becoming a thing of the past now. Why spend hours trying to type something without mistakes when you can hack it in quickly, correct the mistakes easily – usually with the help of an automatic spelling checker – and then have the machine transfer it to paper for you? The simple answer is that, given a choice, you'd use the computer. This book was written entirely on a personal computer, and took only a quarter of the time to write and revise than it would have taken on a typewriter.

Computers can store and manipulate information

Another key use that helps to explain the popularity of computers is in *data manipulation*, i.e. the filing and sorting of information:

- Rather than having to sort through huge card files or filing cabinets to find a list of references matching certain criteria or to retrieve a specific fact or figure, the information can be stored in what is known as a *database*.

- When you need to get to it, you tell the database what you want to know and it will find the answer. This can vary from providing a list of all your customers whom you have not contacted for six months, through to providing the component number and cost of a specific part needed to repair a car engine.

- If you make sure that all the letters you send are typed on a word processor, then a database can keep an exact copy of all of them for future reference and sort through them all for you in moments, finding the ones that you need.

Computers can process numbers

Although word processing and databases are the two commonest business uses for computers, there are still a great number of other vitally important functions that they can perform.

Spreadsheets are designed to allow the storage and manipulation of numbers and numerical information. They can generate graphs, tables and trends to any required specification, perform complicated analytical functions, and work out further data from the numbers that are entered, such as profit/loss totals, yearly summaries, or even complicated mathematical equations. Accountancy is another area where the computer can do almost all the work. A careful blend of database, spreadsheet and word processor, a good *accounts program* is able to prepare all your financial data and paperwork for you at the click of a button. As long as you keep the computer up to date on your expenditure and income, it will be able to offer you expense breakdowns, cashflow predictions, account balances, and even tell you exactly what to put on your tax returns.

Computers can become PAs

Time Management is an increasingly popular use for computers. This allows the machine to work like a combination of secretary, project co-ordinator and personal organiser.

- It can keep a complete record of meetings and engagements, remind you of them safely in advance, and let you know what material you'll need with you at the time.

- You can keep track of the priority of different pieces of work, so that you know which is the most important thing to be getting on with.

- Deadlines can be managed effectively, and you can keep a full record of your personal contacts without having to worry that you might lose a notebook.

- Some *Time Management* systems will even let you know how you can improve your productivity, and suggest changes in the way you organise things.

Computers for publishing

The last of the common uses for computers in offices is *Desktop Publishing*, also known as **DTP**. This involves the manipulation of words and pictures into a finished document that is then ready to print and distribute.

- Photographic, hand-drawn and computer-generated images can be enhanced, altered, made larger or smaller, or tinkered with in dozens of ways until they are exactly as you want them. They can then be laid out into a document, and text added in blocks, columns, tables or paragraphs along with boxes, lines, graphs, charts and logos.

- Everything can be moved around until the graphic design of the document is perfect. Once it is in place, it can be transferred to paper there and then or sent to a commercial printer. It can even be copied onto transparent plastic sheets for display on an overhead projector.

- DTP is now used for the production of everything from reports and presentations to magazines, newspapers and books.

Computers can communicate

As I mentioned earlier, office applications are only one area of strength for personal computers. Another major use is in the field of communications. As international trade barriers become less of an obstacle and the economy becomes more global, good communication facilities are increasingly important.

- A British organisation may well commission a product design from an Australian designer, have the parts made in Korea and then assembled in Mexico for eventual shop sale in America, and have payment going through a holding company in the Cayman Islands for banking in Switzerland.

- In modern business, good access to communications is vital. A personal computer can easily replace a fax machine, so that messages can be word-processed, laid out using DTP and sent straight to another computer with the same capability.

- Networking allows many computers to be linked together so that information can be exchanged almost immediately. Networks may be in the immediate area, known as *Local Area*, but they can also be worldwide, known as *Wide Area*. The majority are private, for the use of a specific company only, but the most important network currently in existence is the *Internet*.

Computers like electronic mail

Like any other network, the Internet is made up of computers linked together. Unlike other networks, there are tens of millions of computers connected to the Internet by leased lines, special trunk cables and telephone connections. Each of them can communicate directly or indirectly with each of the others. Most serious businesses now have a connection to the Internet. *Electronic Mail* is the name given to the system of sending a text message to another person who is linked to the Internet. Almost all networks allow electronic mail (often shortened to **email**) to be passed around. Each of the Internet's millions of users is able to send and receive email from any of the others almost immediately, making it a communication device second in importance only to the telephone.

Computer chat

As well as email, most networks (including the Internet) allow people to exchange messages with each other, in pairs or groups, which are transmitted instantly. This is known by the general term of *Chatting*. It allows people thousands of miles apart to get together and have discussions and conferences without having to travel. Some chatting facilities can now transmit pictures and sound across a network, making telephones almost redundant and eliminating the burden of long distance phone charges. In almost all the developed countries (and a good percentage of the less developed ones), a personal computer can be connected to the Internet by a local telephone call, and once you are connected, you can send messages and gain access to the whole network from that one local call.

Computers for leisure

Personal computers are also widely used for leisure purposes. The home computer market first started with machines that were only really good for playing games on, and although this trend has moved away from the personal computer and towards special games stations, a lot of people still value their computers for entertainment purposes.

- These games range from puzzles and tactical simulations through to tests of reflex and nerve (the so-called 'Shoot-em-Ups') and even interactive movies, where you decide how the plot of a film unfolds and what happens.

- As might be expected, there are also a lot of group-based games that can be played over networks, particularly the Internet. This can range from simply playing someone distant at chess through to *Multi-User Games* (*MUGs* or *MUDs*), where hundreds of people get together to create the illusion that they are all living inside an ever-evolving story with its own plots, adventures, rivalries, dangers and romances.

- Other people connect up to public-access chatting facilities, find a group discussing something interesting and just join in, rather like amateur radio enthusiasts do.

Computers for education

Finally, computers also have a significant role to play in education. The ability to combine movie clips, still pictures, text and sound together makes personal computers excellent learning aids.

- Using the tools developed for businesses, knowledge can be stored, searched and cross-referenced into powerful and captivating electronic encyclopaedias, reference works and primers for specific subjects.

- Some teaching is achieved through play, and many young children learn the first principles of mathematics, language and science with the help of professionally designed computer games.

- At the other end of the educational spectrum, special simulations are available to provide complex help to teach you a new language, a musical instrument and even how to cook well.

- Special simulations are available to provide realistic job training that does not have disastrous consequences when things go wrong. Flight simulators have been used by the aircraft industry for years as a safe and convenient way of training pilots and other airline staff without endangering life. Military organisations, power plant supervisors, trainee doctors, engineers and a wide variety of scientists use other simulations.

To summarise

Computers are already more important to everyday life than most people realise. They are astonishingly versatile and can rapidly make themselves indispensable both around the office and around the home.

For a great many people, the question is not 'Do I need a personal computer?' but 'Which personal computer do I need?' This book will go on to explain what the various options are when buying a computer, what 'extras' are available and what difference it all makes.

Chapter 2

The Computer Itself

Most of the time, a personal computer comes in three separate parts:

- the display screen (known as the *monitor*);
- the keyboard;
- the console that contains the computer itself.

Portable computers of all sizes have all three sections fused together, so that the machine can be carried around easily, and a few old computers still have the keyboard built into the console that holds the circuits, but these cases are the exception.

Personal computers fall into two main types:

- IBM PC and compatible machines (*PCs*),
- Apple Macintosh (*Macs*).

All machines in the same family can, in theory, swap information freely between each other, use the same types of parts, and run the same *software*. Each individual bit of software is called a *program*.

Upgrading your computer

Almost every part of a modern computer can be removed and replaced by the owner, providing that you are careful and have clear instructions. This means that when you need to increase the power of your computer, you can do so by buying parts to add or swap into your existing machine without having to buy a completely new one. This process is known as *upgrading* and is useful for keeping up with technological developments.

When you need to add some new hardware onto your machine, the new part is held in something called an *expansion slot*. Each machine will have a certain number of free slots, either called *ISA* slots or *PCI Card* slots.

If you are expecting to make lots of changes to your computer's insides, then you should make sure that you have at least two or three free expansion slots. Because personal computers are so easy to upgrade and technology is moving so quickly, every different part inside a computer can come in many different versions, made by many different manufacturers, to a variety of qualities and speeds. That is why the adverts are so complicated; there is so much that varies from machine to machine. There is no such thing as the 'standard' personal computer, and even if you asked ten different dealers to describe the bits that would go into the best possible machine, you would still get ten different answers.

Inside your computer

There are a small number of key elements inside your computer console that are very important, these are:

- the *processor*
- the *RAM*
- the *hard disk*

The processor

The processor is the true computer. This is, in effect, the brain, the part that sits at the core of the machine and works out how to do what you tell it to do and what all the other different parts ought to be doing in order to obey you. The better the processor, the faster the machine will perform calculations, respond to your commands, update graphical images on the monitor, and so on. There are two elements that combine to tell you how good a processor is: the *type* and the *speed*. Processor speed is a simple matter; it is measured in megahertz (MHz), and the higher it is, the better.

The IBM PC

The current top-of-the-range PC processor is the **Pentium IV**© (a registered trademark of the Intel Corporation), or **586** (if it wasn't made by Intel). In order of decreasing quality, the other PC processor types are: 586, 486 (DX processors are better than SX ones), 386, 286 and 8086. The 386, 286 and 8086, although considered to be obsolete with very little new software available that will run on them, are still useful tools for basic computing.

Apple Macintosh™ computers

The current processor range for Apple Macs is the iMac G4 preceded by the iMac G3. The machines are not always described in terms of their processor. Many Macs are described in both adverts and magazines as 'Power PCs' or even just 'PCs', because the abbreviation simply stands for 'Personal Computer'.

In this book, I will stick to PC meaning an IBM compatible machine. Some Macs can be forced to run the same software as IBM compatible machines, but only the ones described as 'Power PCs'. IBM machines cannot run software written for the Mac.

When buying a machine whether it is an IBM PC or an Apple Mac, the rule is simple: get the best processor that you can afford. While you may not need buckets of speed, software manufacturers tend to concentrate their efforts on the higher edge of the market, and if you buy a cheaper processor, you may find that in six or twelve months' time, your machine is now too slow to run the latest releases. Saving money on a processor is a false economy. Don't worry too much if you can't afford an **Intel**© **Pentium**©, though; like everything else, the processor can be upgraded at a later date for a fraction of the cost of a new machine.

Accessing and saving information

Apart from the processor, the other vital consideration in a machine is its memory. For computers, memory comes in various forms:

RAM – stands for Random Access Memory, and is the area in which the user stores instructions for the machine to obey. Any program, piece of software or instruction needs to be put into RAM (this is known as *loading*) before the computer can do anything with it, and it all takes up a certain amount of space once it is inside. When you load a piece of software, it goes into RAM. When you type information into that software, it too goes into still more RAM.

Any information held in RAM can be stored for later recall, which is known as *saving*. On modern machines, there isn't much that you can do without first loading one or more programs. In fact, when you turn a personal computer on, it automatically loads several programs into RAM that allow it to talk to you. For almost all tasks that you want it to do, you will load more programs, and you will tell these what you want the machine to do and what information you want it to work with. You should think of programs as negotiators between you and the computer; you tell the program what you want and then it goes off and explains your requirements to the computer. A program takes up a certain amount of RAM, and if the amount it needs is more than your machine has, then you will not be able to load that program.

Hard Disk Memory – Obviously, programs have to be stored somewhere so that the computer can find them before they can be loaded into RAM, and you will also usually want to store the information that you enter into them. When you turn a computer off, everything in the RAM is lost. It would be no use having a database if you had to type all the data in every time you wanted to use it, so data is saved for later use. With personal computers, information and programs are generally stored on the hard disk (sometimes abbreviated to *HD* or *HDD* in adverts).

Any particular hard disk has a certain amount of memory that it can hold. You can think of it a bit like a library; you can fit a certain number of books on the shelves to look at later, but no more. When you want to read a book, you have to take it from the shelf and open it before you can start reading. If the book isn't in the library, you can't take it out and read it. The computer is the same; it cannot load a program if the program is not stored where it can read it, and it cannot put more programs and information on the hard disk than will fit into it.

Floppy Disk Memory – The majority of computers can also use floppy disks (or, more commonly, just *disks*) in the same way. These are the 3.5-inch squares of firm plastic, usually blue, beige or black that most people are familiar with. They work in exactly the same way as a hard disk, except that they have far less room on them. If a hard disk is a library, a floppy disk is a small bookshelf. Unlike hard disks, however, floppies are not wired up to your machine but inserted and removed from a special *disk drive* slot in the computer.

In advertising, this is often referred to by the initials *FD* or *FDD*. They are also cheap to buy and can be stored away from your computer, so they are normally used for holding information that you will not want very often and for keeping backup copies of your data in case the main computer is stolen, destroyed or breaks down.

Optical Disk Drives – The compact disk is an ideal storage medium for many kinds of users:

- □ graphics professionals who need an inexpensive way to store several hundred megabytes of scanned image data for easy retrieval;

- □ multimedia authors who encode digital video onto Video CDs, or create multimedia 'demo disks' of their clients' products;

- □ those who want to duplicate existing CDs.

Recordable rewriteable CD-ROM technology (CD-R/CD-RW) – which allows users to record their own CDs and play them back on stereos or PCs is steadily becoming the storage platform of choice among PC manufacturers and consumers.

Zip drives – The zip drive is a storage device manufactured and trademarked by Iomega. The zip drive is capable of storing 100 megabytes and 250 megabytes on disks similar in size and appearance to standard 1.4 megabyte floppy disks, but zip drives cannot read or write standard floppy disks.

The zip drive has become the almost universal choice for intermediate-size removable storage, in no small part because there are versions of the drive to accommodate every taste. Various versions of the zip can connect to the computer via the parallel port, SCSI port, USB, IEEE 1394 (Firewire) or internally via the IDE interface. There are also expansion-bay versions of the zip drive compatible with many popular laptop brands.

Memory considerations

All memory is measured in units known as *bytes*. The storage size of programs is usually measured in kilobytes (thousands of bytes, referred to as *KB* or just K).

- □ A million bytes, 1000 kilobytes, is called a megabyte (referred to as *MB*, M or *Meg*). Most current software is now over 30MB in size.

- □ A thousand megabytes make a Gigabyte (GB, G or *Gig*). 1GB = 1,000MB = 1,000,000KB = 1,000,000,000 bytes.

Hard Disks are measured in either GB or MB. Some programs are so large that they now need over 100MB of your Hard Drive disk space. For practical purposes, if you want to use up-to-date software, you will need an absolute minimum 8GB Hard Drive. A 20GB Hard Drive is considered a comfortable amount of space. RAM is nearly always measured in MB. 64MB of RAM is fine but the ideal is 512MB of RAM. Standard size floppy disks are now 1.44MB.

Memory chips

A memory chip is a chip that holds programs and data either temporarily or permanently. The major categories of memory chips are *RAMs* and *ROMs*.

RAM Chips – RAM stands for random-access memory. Random- access memory holds the data or instructions that the CPU (central processing unit) is presently processing. The type of primary storage is RAM. That is, a collection of RAM chips builds primary storage.

Whenever a CPU writes data or instructions to RAM, it wipes out the previous contents of RAM, and when a CPU reads data or instructions from RAM, it keeps their contents.

ROM Chips – ROM stands for read-only memory. A ROM chip is a memory chip that stores instructions and data permanently. Its contents are placed into the ROM chip at the time of manufacture and cannot be modified by the user. A CPU can read and retrieve the instructions and data from the ROM chip, but it cannot change the contents in ROM.

In summary

- The terms KB, MB and GB are units that measure memory, which is a bit like the space on a desk.

- RAM is the computer's working space.

- ROM contains data or instructions for running your computer. It is provided by the manufacturer, and cannot be altered.

- The hard disk (or HD) is where you store software programs and data that you have created.

- MHz is a unit that represents the speed of the processor, the computer's 'brain'.

- The floppy disks enable you to transfer information from one computer to another or keep as a storage medium. You should attempt to buy a processor that complements the memory you will have.

- For a PC, you should have a Pentium running at 1 to 2GHz.

- If you do not need to use up-to-date software and just want an old machine for simple tasks such as basic word processing, then you can get by with something as low as a 286 processor, 1MB of RAM (or even less; 512KB is the minimum possible) and a 20MB Hard Drive.

Cache memory

At this point, it is also worth mentioning something known as *cache memory*. It is quite technical, and you don't need to worry about exactly what it means or how it works. A cache is a specially designed buffer storage used to improve your computer's performance by reducing the time it takes to access instructions and data that are likely to be needed for the next operation by the processor. The cache copies frequently accessed data and instructions from the main memory or secondary storage disks.

Simply, the more cache memory the machine has, the faster it can run. If you are buying a Pentium, a **burst-mode pipeline** cache is worth obtaining. Remember that everything on a personal computer can be upgraded and it is relatively simple to fit more RAM and a second Hard Drive to your computer later on. The machine that you buy can always be improved later.

The keyboard

There are, of course, a whole host of other details that you can specify on a personal computer that you are buying. As mentioned earlier, the machine generally comes in three sections; the *monitor*, the *keyboard* and the *console*. The monitor and keyboard have as many different varieties as everything else does. Unless you are a trained typist with a specific preference for one sort of keyboard or another, you should make sure that you get a standard, 102-key model with your machine. Trends come and go for keyboards, and fads can spring up, like the current 'ergonomic' keyboards which separate out the keys into two halves, so that you are forced to use both hands. These can be difficult and uncomfortable for beginners and they are not recommended. Stick with the basic configuration – a typewriter-style main panel, a data entry numberpad panel, a set of directional arrows between the two panels with a block of special keys above it, and a row of function keys along the top. You can always purchase a special keyboard later if you discover that you need to be able to type at 120 words per minute.

The monitor

Computer monitors, the screens that the computer produces images upon, are often surrounded with unnecessary detail in adverts. The two main considerations are screen size and colour display.

Screen size

Monitors, like televisions, are measured in size from the top right corner to the bottom left. This often makes them sound bigger than they are, as many people assume that the size is the height of the screen or its width.

Most monitors are either 14", 15", 17" or 19"; frankly, the extra inch makes a big difference. If you are going to be doing a lot of detailed graphics design or DTP document layout, then you might want to consider investing in a larger monitor.

Colour display

Super VGA is a very high resolution standard that displays up to 65,536 colours, supporting 16.8 million colours at 800 by 600 pixels and 256 colours at 1024 by 768 pixels.

A high-priced super VGA allows 1280 by 1024 pixels. Larger monitors (17" or 21" and larger) with a high resolution of 1600 by 1280 pixels are available.

The graphics card

A significant factor with a monitor is to make sure that it can cope with displaying the pictures from your machine. The quality and complexity of these images is decided by the quality of the *graphics card* (sometimes abbreviated to *gfx card*) in your machine. This is like a little bit of extra brain for the computer, which does all the work involving pictures and putting them onto the monitor. Every machine that can support picture output has one. They have all sorts of dreadful technical terms and abbreviations surrounding them, but they can also be described by the biggest *resolution* and *colour palette* that they can cope with.

Every image produced by a computer is made up of tiny little dots that can be one of a wide range of colours. The better your graphics card is, the more dots it can put on the screen and the greater the range of colours there can be.

- ☐ The number of dots is called the resolution.
- ☐ The range of colours is the palette.

Resolution is always described as the number of dots in a horizontal line multiplied by the number of dots in a vertical line, such as 640 x 480. This is because the numbers get too huge to remember and work with easily if they are totalled up. The palette is also often added after a second multiplication sign, so that the standard graphics capacity for a minimum new PC can be written as: 800 x 600 x 256 colours.

There are several standard graphic combinations, called *modes*. At the time of writing, the current minimum specification is called **SVGA**, which is the 800 x 600 x 256 colours mentioned above. An older standard mode was **VGA**, which is only 640 x 480 x 16 colours and is not sufficient to run modern games. Totally outdated graphics modes include **EGA**, which can only manage 4 colours, and **ANSI** and **ASCII**, which cannot cope with any graphics at all, just text.

Unless you only want to use your machine for word processing, make sure that both the graphics card and the monitor can run SVGA graphics. There are many semi-standard graphic modes that are better than SVGA but they are not yet fully accepted. Having said that, the greater the resolution and palette that your graphics card and monitor can cope with, the better placed you will be to cope with advances in the industry. All you need to do is to make sure that your monitor can cope with whatever your graphics card can throw at it.

Monitor refresh rates and emissions

You will find the terms *Non-Interlaced*, *Refresh Rate* and *Low Emission* associated with monitor advertising. The refresh rate is fairly important – it represents how fast the monitor redraws the screen and can be as low as 43MHz. For detailed graphics, you should try to make sure that this rate is at least 73MHz.

The other details aren't totally irrelevant (you don't want an interlaced monitor, but nearly all of them are non-interlaced now), but the only one that you might want to consider is low emission, which means that the screen has been partially shielded against energy leakage.

There is a current debate as to whether computer screens leak out energy or not and, if they do, whether this is a health risk or not. It is a popular target for scare mongering journalists, and so many companies now make partially shielded monitors to cash in on the fear caused by the possibility. They are also known as radiation-shielded, low-radiation and a range of other fairly obvious terms. If you are concerned about the possibilities, try to choose such a monitor.

To summarise

The current minimum specification for monitors and graphics cards is usually written in adverts as a *'17" CRT SVGA Colour Monitor'* and a *'66MB [Company Name] Graphics Card'*. You should check that you get at least this. If you are going to need to work with high-quality graphical images or do a lot of layout or design, you should try to get the best monitor and graphics card that you can afford.

Portable computers

You will often find computers referred to by the size of their case. The main split is between those machines that you can use while travelling, known in general as *portables*, and those that you cannot, known as *desktops*. Portable computers are far more expensive than desktops, and are usually less powerful. They have small screens and keyboards built into the inside of the case, which opens up to allow you to use it. All portables nowadays have a removable hard disk and a removable floppy disk drive. Typing on the smaller portables can be difficult. While all portables can be plugged into an electricity supply, they also run on rechargeable batteries. Battery time varies greatly and can be as little as two hours in some cases. On the plus side however, portables do allow you access to your computer no matter where you are.

Palmtop computers

Portable computers vary in size. The smallest ones are known as *palmtops*. These are just about the same size as an electronic personal organiser and will fit snugly into the inside pocket of a jacket. The keys and screen are obviously very small, but some of these machines are surprisingly powerful. They do not have enough battery power for either floppy or hard disks and instead store information on special cards, known as *PC cards* (or, previously, *PCMCIA cards*), or special RAM known as *Static RAM*. The main advantage of palmtops is obvious: you can carry them around in a pocket without really noticing, and they are particularly popular with people who are looking for an expensive status symbol.

Notebook computers

The next size of portable computer is the *notebook*, which is defined as being, at most, as wide and broad as a sheet of A4 paper (29.7cm by 21cm) and 10cm tall. It is still possible to include full-size keys on a notebook, but the screen is smaller and less versatile than that of a desktop. The typical minimum spec for a notebook is a 13.3" LCD screen with a 4 or 8MB graphics card with a maximum resolution of 1024x768. They also make heavy use of PC cards and Static RAM, but can include a floppy drive and a hard disk.

Laptop computers

The next largest personal computers are *laptops* and are now generally considered to be somewhat inferior. These vary quite a lot in size, from being just a bit bigger and heavier than a notebook to being almost the same size and weight as a well-packed briefcase.

Docking stations

A docking station is a device to which a portable computer can be connected so that it can be used like a desktop computer when you are not out and about.

While this can be extremely useful, allowing you to use your machine normally most of the time and then carry it with you conveniently when you have to, the computer itself is a portable and has the associated limitations of speed, power and price.

Portable versus desktop computer

One of the most serious problems with portable computers is that unlike their larger cousins, they are not as easy or cheap to upgrade. Components have to be specially produced for most portables, often in special versions that take less power to operate and so are quite a lot more expensive. The internal structure of the machine is also usually cramped and so fitting the upgrade can be a lot more complex.

In general, you should only consider a portable computer if you expect to need it while on the move. *Desktop* computers have broad, deep cases that can be anything up to 20 or 30 cm tall and tend to have the assorted drives and lights set into the front. The monitor is usually placed on top of the case, with the keyboard just in front of it, so that the machine almost seems to be in one piece.

There is a variation to this pattern, which is known as the *tower*. A tower case is the same shape as a desktop one, but it is designed to be placed on its side, so that the front of the machine is tall and narrow rather than flat and wide. Towers are usually placed on the floor beside the table or desk that holds the monitor and keyboard. There are no other real practical differences between the two types and they are jointly considered to be the standard kind of personal computer.

Workstations and terminals

It is also sensible to mention two different types of machine, called *workstations* and *terminals*. Neither type is designed to operate on its own; instead, they are connected by cables to a much larger, distant computer – the type that needs a system operator to keep it running. Terminals have just enough electronics to talk to the main computer, whereas workstations have far more circuitry. Many personal computers can also pretend to be terminals and workstations if they need to, but the reverse is not necessarily true.

In summary

The computer itself consists of three physical chunks: the monitor, the keyboard and the console. Inside the case, you'll have several vital elements, including the RAM, hard disk, floppy drive, processor, cache and graphics card.

If you have a desktop computer, it should come with a **mouse** (a small box with buttons that you can push around over a flat surface, and is used in many software programs to move a little pointer around on the monitor screen) or, if it is a portable, there may be a *'mouse-ball'*, *'tracker-ball'* or *'finger pad'* built into the case, which will serve the same purpose.

There are plenty of other bits and bobs, but you don't need to worry about them too much. All of these bits and pieces are connected directly or indirectly to a piece of circuit board known as a *motherboard*, which is what all the different components fit into.

The console itself can come in a variety of shapes and sizes, depending on where you'll need to use the machine. Of all of the bits and pieces, the most important internal bits to spend extra money on are the processor, RAM and hard disk.

Multimedia systems

One of the most popular improvements to personal computers at the moment – so common that most machines now feature this as standard – is to turn them into multimedia systems. This allows the machine to work with a number of different forms of data that were not traditionally associated with computers.

The most common type of multimedia upgrade is to include a *sound card* and a pair of small audio speakers. To complete the system you will also need an *Optical Disk Drive*.

An optical disk is a disk that can store data which can be written to and read by a laser beam. Optical disks do not spin like conventional music CDs in a CD player. It does not need to move access arms or read/write heads, because a laser beam can be moved electronically. The storage capacity of the disks is considerably greater than their magnetic disk counterparts, and optical disk storage may eventually replace all magnetic tape and disk storage.

There are three forms of optical disks available, and are better known as:

- Compact Disk – Read Only Memory (CD-ROM)
- Digital Video Disk *(DVD)*
- Compact Disk Write Only/Rewritable Drives (CD-R/CD-RW)

CD-ROM

- CD-ROM is an optical disk storage that contains text, graphics and hi-fi stereo sound.
- A CD-ROM is a 4.75-inch optical disk that can store around 650MB of data.
- A CD-ROM is almost the same as the music CD, but uses different forms of track for data.
- A CD-ROM drive can read music CDs, but a CD player cannot read CD-ROMs.
- A CD-ROM is a read-only disk that cannot be written on or erased by the user.

DVD

- DVD disks can store between 4.7 and 17GB (that's 4,700-17,000MB) on a disk the same size as a CD. This is up to 26 times more data than a conventional CD-ROM or CD-R/CD-RW disk.

- DVD disks can also store complete films with better than VHS quality and 'surround-sound'.

CD-R

- A CD-R disk is an optical disk that can be written on just once by the user and then cannot be overwritten.

- It is ideal for archiving information, because it can be read many times, but the data cannot be erased.

- The storage capacity of CD-R disks ranges from 400 MB to 6.4 GB.

CD-RW

- A CD-RW disk is an optical disk that can be erased and written on repeatedly.

- An erasable optical disk has a great deal of data capacity. It can store up to 4.6 GB.

- An erasable optical disk functions like a magnetic disk and has huge capacity, so it will eventually replace the magnetic disk in the future.

Sound cards

The sound card is a piece of electronics that allows the computer to produce a far greater variety and number of sounds than its own built-in speaker can cope with. Sound cards vary in their processing power. This is referred to in terms of how many *bits* (1s or 0s) the card can calculate simultaneously. The worst cards are described as 16-bit, with the standard ones being 32-bit. The next step up, 64-bit sound cards, are now in common use. Some sound cards are MIDI-compatible, which allows them to work with professional music production equipment, and allows the card to convert certain types of data into recognisable music. This can be very important for a minority of people, but will prove largely irrelevant for most users.

The popularity of multimedia systems has grown as the range of DVD titles available has grown. These are often visually and audibly stunning, combining clean, sharp graphics with fully-textured sound and smooth animation. This sort of software is used mainly for films, reference works and educational programs, but there is also a growing selection of highly impressive games. If the funds are available, it is wise to purchase a multimedia computer. As software programs continue getting larger, optical storage disks are increasingly becoming the most viable way of selling them to end-users. There is a danger of systems without a CD Drive being left on the sidelines.

Chapter 3

Printers

Printers are usually considered to be the first add-on, or *peripheral*, that a new owner should obtain. While there are a wide variety of different types, they all have the same purpose – to transfer information from the computer onto paper. Some of the cheaper printers can only manage simple text, while the most expensive can produce pages that are easily as good as any glossy magazine, advertising brochure or photograph. Without printers, the personal computer would never have risen to the importance that it holds today. What use would it be to be able to organise and edit text in a word processor if it was not then possible to transfer the document into print?

Daisywheel printers

The earliest printers worked in a very similar way to typewriters. The computer would tell the printer what letter to type next, then the printer would strike a metal key against a ribbon in order to mark the paper. Changing the way in which the keys were organised increased speed. *Daisywheel printers*, which are still available, had all the letter keys in a circle around a central spoke. When the machine had to type a certain letter, it would spin the circle of keys until the correct one was nearest the paper and then punch down with it.

Other machines used a ball with the keys embossed upon it or, for the fastest machines, a huge drum made up of lots of free-moving sections. Each section on these *drum printers* had all the letters on it, so that the machine looked at the whole line of text and span all the sections to print the entire line in one go.

Of course, any printer that relied on striking metal keys against an ink ribbon was only able to print letters and symbols that it had the correct key for. Printing out lines and pictures was unthinkable. These machines were large and noisy – many had to be kept in special soundproof boxes – and, by today's standards, very slow. They were in existence long before personal computers and home computers were available and so were mostly used by institutions and large companies.

Dot matrix printers

Things were shaken up with the invention of a new type of printer. Computers create the letters that you see on the monitor screen by filling in dots on a grid. Nowadays that grid is extremely fine, but a few years ago, all letters were drawn up on a grid just eight dots across and eight dots tall.

A new type of printer was developed that did not have a set of metal keys, but instead had a grid of small, blunt square rods. Any letter that needed to be printed could now be printed by hitting the correct pattern of rods against the ink ribbon. Better still, as long as the computer could tell the printer which rods to press, they did not have to be limited to just letters. Lines could be printed as easily as letters; it was just a matter of working out which rods to punch down at what point.

These printers were called *dot matrix*, because the grid that punched rods at the paper, the print head, was made up of a matrix of dots. They were almost as loud and slow as daisywheel printers, and the grids were so clumsy that their work looked ugly and artificial. Just as the grids that computers use to show pictures on our monitors have grown finer and finer, so have the grids used on printers to print letters, pictures, charts and everything else.

Almost all of the modern printers use the same idea of making a shape inside a grid and then transferring it onto the paper, including laser printers and inkjet printers, but they are different in the way that they do the actual printing.

Inkjet and bubblejet printers

Inkjet and *bubblejet* printers are normally thought of as the next stage up in printer technology. Rather than pressing rods down onto an inked ribbon, inkjets have a cartridge of liquid dye that they squirt through a tiny nozzle onto the paper. They still form their letters and images in dots like dot matrix printers do, but they actually push ink into the paper rather than press a ribbon onto it.

As long as you make sure that the printer has a supply of ink, the work it produces stays consistently dark, which has never been true of dot matrixes. Ribbons do not get used up evenly and can start to dry out, so the output from a dot matrix printer can quickly become uneven and even patchy at times. It takes a certain time for the ink to dry after an inkjet has just printed a page – the exact amount depends on the paper and the quality of the ink cartridge – and although they have improved a lot in recent years, the pages that they produce tend to smudge if you are not careful when you touch them. If the paper absorbs the ink too easily, the letters will also blur.

Wax transfer printers were popular for a short time and worked in almost exactly the same way as inkjets, but although their pages did not smudge quite as much once they had dried, there were other associated problems.

Thermal printers

During the home computer boom of the early 1980s, a class of printer known as *thermal printers* was popular. These were very cheap, because of the poor output. Rather than worrying about ink, they used very hot rods to burn dots into special silvery rolls of paper. The printer could not use normal paper at all, which was a big handicap. Their quality was appalling, even by the standards of the time, and although greatly advanced modern versions can occasionally be found they are, mostly, extinct.

Laser printers

The type of printer commonly found in personal computing is the *laser printer*. These are without doubt the most popular, and most people who use an inkjet or dot matrix printer do so because they are unable to afford a laser. They do not actually have anything to do with laser technology, but were given the name on the grounds that their output was as sharp as if it had been burnt in by a laser – compared to blocky dot matrixes and blurred inkjets, anyway.

The paper is held against an electromagnetic drum, which then magnetises the points that it wants to come out coloured. A jet of powdered ink, called toner, is shot at the page and it sticks to the points that have been magnetised. The toner is then melted (or *fused*) onto the paper. The edges and letters come out sharp, the fused toner does not blur or smudge, and the overall effect can look very close to professional printing; better, even, on some expensive lasers. The down side is the cost – the toner is expensive and gets used up quite quickly if you regularly do a lot of printing. The machines themselves also tend to be more expensive than inkjets and dot matrixes.

The plotter

One completely different type of printer is known as the *plotter*. This does not reduce its output to grids, but instead has a pen on a computer-controlled arm that is told how to draw lines so as to recreate the text or image that is desired. They are far slower than the other types of printer, but can be far more precise. The pages that they output can be good enough to look hand-drawn, which is not true of other types of printer. They are usually used to produce charts, technical diagrams and other similar high-accuracy data and are far more commonly found in laboratories or design and architecture workrooms than in offices.

Printer speed

The quality of inkjets and laser printers is generally measured by two different factors, how fast they print and how fine their grids are. Speed is normally measured in the number of pages that the machine can print in one minute. Although laser printers print an entire line at one time, whereas dot matrixes and inkjets have to print a single block at one time, lasers are not always the fastest.

The time it will take will depend a lot on how exactly how much of the page needs to be inked, so plain text prints faster than complicated graphics, which need to be converted to dots. When speeds are given in adverts, they will nearly always be for a page of plain text. This page is assumed to be A4, Letter, or whatever your national standard office-paper page size is. This speed is called *Pages Per Minute* and is always abbreviated to **PPM**. Most cheaper laser printers can manage between 12 and 20 PPM.

Print quality

The measure of quality is the number of dots that the printer can fit into its grid. This is now calculated by the number of points that the printer can cram into one inch and is referred to by the term **dpi**, or *Dots Per Inch*. The more dots the printer can get into one inch, the better the quality of the work it produces. Cheaper laser printers have a smaller dpi rating; it is possible to buy a 600dpi laser printer now for about the same as a reasonable inkjet. To get true letter-quality output though, you will need a printer with 1200dpi or better, and this is fairly standard now.

Some laser printers use a special technology called *edge enhancement* to effectively double their actual dpi. They are cheaper than the machines with genuinely higher dpi and are almost the same quality. By comparison, dot matrix printers are measured by the number of rods that the machine has in its grid – known as *pins* – and the number of *characters* that it can print in any one second. A character is a single letter, number, symbol or gap. The more pins that a dot matrix printer has, the sharper and tighter its output. There are two standard types: 9-pin and 24-pin. Astonishingly, 9-pin dot matrix printers are almost exactly the same as they were fifteen years ago, and their work looks it, but they are an extremely cheap option. The more expensive 24-pin dot matrix printers also use similarly old technology, but their output is closer to typewriter quality. The term **NLQ**, which stands for *Near-Letter Quality*, is often used to describe this higher level of printing.

Paper feed methods

Printers obtain their paper to print upon in different ways. Many dot matrix machines use spiked wheels to drag paper past the print grid. This means that they can only use special paper with perforated hole-punched strips on each side, known as *fanfold paper*. This tends to be fairly cheap and adds to the unpopularity of dot matrix machines. On the other hand, it is perfect for printing labels, which are often sold in fanfold strips.

Most lasers, inkjets and better dot matrixes use a system of *sheet feeding*, and generally use standard photocopier paper unless instructed otherwise. A few cannot store more than one sheet of paper for use at a time, which is a great disadvantage; this is known as *single-sheet* feeding. It is far more common for a printer to have both a single-sheet feeder and a *paper tray*, which will usually hold at least 100 sheets at a time.

Many printers can also be told to print envelopes and smaller paper sizes and some can also fit thinner types of card. Special laser-ready labels and similar products are readily available and work by fitting a more unusual paper shape into the framework of a more normal paper size.

Colour printing

Colour printing is one of the areas that is advancing most rapidly at the moment. Colour laser printing is impractical for the vast majority of users – the costs would simply be too high – and so the choice comes down to either dot matrix or inkjet. In either case, combining dots of three different colours – cyan, magenta and yellow – and sometimes black, generates colour. Each colour requires a separate source, so these machines need three or four different cartridges. If there are only three, then the closest to black that the printer can manage is a dark grey and this is both very slow and expensive. Even with four cartridges, printing colour images is slow and the quality does not approach photographs.

Colour dot matrixes use strips that have banded colour and are far faster, but are also poorer quality. The equipment necessary to print convincing colour images is extremely expensive and is not very different to hooking a colour photocopier to your computer.

The very latest inkjet printers, however, use super *'Micropiezo'* inkjet technology with colour and black cartridges ready to print up to 12 pages black and 11.7 pages colour at a maximum 2880x720 dpi. These printers are claimed to have photo quality when printing on specially coated photographic paper.

Deciding which printer to buy

When buying a printer, you need to consider how important the quality of the output needs to be. If you will be using the computer to print formal or business-related documents, you should attempt to purchase a laser printer as they are definitely superior. If you cannot afford one, then get an inkjet. If you only need a printer for keeping paper copies of data or for sending personal letters, then a dot matrix might be sufficient. Printers are difficult to upgrade significantly, so providing that the need is there, it is often worth going for the best one that you can afford.

Chapter 4

Modems

A *modem* is a clever gadget that lets your computer talk down a telephone line to another computer or, often, to a fax machine. The modem is currently going through a surge of popularity due mainly to the *Internet*, and the ability to send and receive *emails*. Modems work by changing information into sound and then sending that sound across a phone link to another modem, which turns it back into information again.

The name 'modem' is a contraction of the term MOdulator/DEModulator, which is a technical description of what it does. For the small-scale user, a modem is the only practical way to connect their machine to a distant one. While this may not be a major concern for the average computer owner, it is important if you want to connect to the Internet.

Fax modems

One of the main uses of a modem in a small business environment is as a substitute fax machine. With the help of a piece of software known as a *fax emulator*, the computer becomes able to send and receive faxes. Because a modem can only transmit information that is stored inside the computer, it cannot send a paper document for you like a normal fax would; instead, you use a word processor or desktop publishing package to create the document inside the computer. Then, rather than printing it out onto a printer to fax it to someone else, you send it to the fax emulator software, tell it which machine to send it to, and it will be printed out on the fax machine at the other end.

You can also tell the modem and fax emulator to act as a fax machine for incoming calls. They will answer the telephone in the same way as a fax machine would, and when a connection is established, the computer will receive the information. Again, it will not automatically print the fax out for you unless you have previously told it to; instead, it will store a picture of the information that you have been sent, putting it safely onto your hard disk. When you want to read the fax, you just call up the picture and read.

Coping as they do with both incoming and outgoing faxes, modems can save a small business a lot of money. Not all modems can pretend to be faxes in this way, but most of them can, particularly the newer models. For once, the computer industry has come up with a fairly obvious way of describing something, and calls modems with fax ability *fax modems*.

Internal modems

There are, broadly speaking, two styles of modem available: *internal* and *external*. An internal modem is fitted inside your computer, plugged into special slots on the main circuit board. The user can only get to it by opening the computer. All the controls for it are software-based, stored inside programs that are held on your hard disk.

External modems

External modems are separate bits of equipment, small boxes with a long row of lights on the front, that need to be connected to the back of the computer and also to be plugged into the mains electricity supply. Both types of modem also need to be plugged into a telephone socket. For an internal modem, there will be a special phone-cable socket that is set into the back of the computer.

There is a third type of modem, known as a *modem PC card* that can be used in certain portable machines. These are actually slotted into the side of the machine when you want to use them, making them a variation of internal modems. Some of this type of modem can actually work with a digital mobile phone, so that the user is able to stay connected to a distant machine while travelling. This can be very useful for people who need access to office computers while they are out on business, particularly salespeople. It is an expensive way to work, however, because of the cost of mobile telephone charges and of the equipment itself. There is also a risk of the information being copied by someone, because mobile telephone calls are not private and can be intercepted by anyone with a wide-band radio receiver.

External versus internal

There are advantages and disadvantages to both internal and external modems. Internal modems are generally easier to use than external ones. They do not require a power supply of their own, and do not confuse the owner with the barrage of little flashing lights that external modems have. They also tend to be fairly standard and so require little in the way of setting up to get the best performance from them. However, it is these very points that contribute to their weaknesses. Because they are deep inside the computer, it is impossible to examine them closely when things do not seem to be working.

The bank of lights on external modems, confusing and irritating when things work well, is in fact a very useful tool for working out what is wrong. Modems work in quite complicated ways and there are many possible problems. If you can't connect to a computer, it does not mean that the modem is not working: the telephone line could be faulty; you could be trying to connect to a number that does not have a modem at the other end or that is not being answered; the other machine might be having difficulties talking to your modem; or the distant computer itself might be connecting but might not be sending or receiving information.

The bank of lights can prove a vital diagnostic tool when you need to work out where a problem lies. Even if things seem to be working, often the speed at which the other machine talks to you will vary as other people also make requests from it.

Two of the most important lights on an external modem show the passage of information; one flickers as you get information, and the other flickers as you send it. They are called *Rx* and *Tx* respectively, from 'Receive' and 'Transmit'. If things seem to be slow, they will tell you whether the other machine is doing something else for the moment. Obviously, they are unavailable on an internal modem.

There is a far greater variety of external modems than of internal ones. Each one has slightly different internal commands, and so external modems are more complicated to get working. Often, you will need to tell the computer exactly what make of external modem you have. There is no doubt that internal modems are simpler to use, but the price of simplicity is the loss of some control. You have to consider the advantages and disadvantages, and decide for yourself which you prefer.

Modem speeds

The most important factor in the quality of a modem is the speed at which it can send information. The faster your modem works, the less time you have to spend connected to the telephone and, unless you live in the United States and are making a local call, paying phone charges for the privilege. This is a very important consideration. You may think that you are saving money by buying a cheaper, slower modem, but if you use it regularly it will be a false economy.

Baud rates

The speed of modems is described in two different ways and they are fairly interchangeable. The easier of the two ways is to simply say what the modem's maximum speed of passing information actually is. This is measured in *bits per second*, or **bps**. This measurement is called the **baud rate**. As modems have become faster over the years, their speed has increased so much that it is now common to measure the baud rate in thousands of bps, which is written as **Kbps**.

When the first modem became popular on the home market, 300bps was considered a fairly normal speed. To compare it to someone typing, hitting 300bps would mean working at about 7 words a second, or about five times faster than a professional typist. That meant that the modem would keep up with a person putting in information. Nowadays, the fastest modems are hitting 56,000bps – that's an increase of over 18,700% in a decade or so, and represents a theoretical typing rate of some 100,000 words a minute.

This top speed could be written in several different ways in an advert. The possibilities would include **56,580 bps**, **56.5 Kbps**, and even **56K8**. There are several standard slower speeds that you might meet: these are **31.2 Kbps**, **28.8 Kbps**, **14.4 Kbps** and **9.6 Kbps**. Of these slower speeds, the **9.6 Kbps** modems are now obsolete and the **14.4 Kbps** ones have nearly gone the same way.

International standards

Because two modems can only talk to each other if they are both talking at the same speed and using the same format, international standard speeds and formats have been in place for almost as long as there have been modems. As technology advances, new standards are agreed.

Each standard represents a certain level of performance for the modem and so some adverts show the best standard that the modem can reach rather than its top speed. The standards that are currently important are **V90** (56.0 Kbps and 31.2 Kbps), **V34** (28.8 Kbps), and **V32** (14.4 Kbps). Almost all modems can reach all the lower standard speeds that have gone before, so some advertisers will attempt to make inferior machines sound good by including a list of all the older speeds, such as V23, V22 and V21. Furthermore, standard fax types can also be referred to as V17, V27 and V29 (Fax group 3, 2 and 1 transmissions respectively, but do not worry about this), and there is an error-checking and data correction standard known as V42.

Sometimes you will encounter these standards with **bis** or **ter** written after the number, such as **V32bis** or **V42ter**. These represent slight modifications to the base standard and don't really need to be worried about. With modems, it is generally the case that the more standards they include in the advert, the more suspicious you should be.

Hayes compatible

One other term that you might find casually thrown into modem advertising is *'Hayes Compatible'*. This is a standard method that allows the two modems to talk to each other in the first place and to negotiate the speed at which they will communicate. This process is also known as *handshaking*.

In the modern market, it is almost impossible to find a modem that is not Hayes Compatible or that does not have automatic handshaking so, again, these points are fairly trivial and if an advert for a modern modem does not mention them, that does not mean that it doesn't have the facilities.

More relevant to many people will be the fact that some modems are now becoming able to answer a call, decide whether it is a computer, fax machine or person who is on the other end of the line, and route the call to the appropriate place. There are currently no standard descriptions for these abilities so most adverts will have to describe them in plain English. If you think that they could be useful, it is worth consulting a professional for advice as the market is evolving too rapidly at the current time to allow any meaningful comments to be included in this book.

Chapter 5

Scanners

The last group of common personal computer peripherals are *scanners*. These bits of equipment are used to transfer images directly into the computer to be stored, copied into documents or changed around as appropriate. Pretty much any flat surface can be scanned, from ancient works of art, photographs and photocopies, to the palm of your hand.

Scanners get their information in much the same way as photocopiers do, running a bright light along the surface and working out the whole picture by adding lots of small strips together. Any time you see a photograph image on a computer screen, you can be certain that it was originally scanned into a computer.

As a piece of equipment, scanners are most useful for people who want to produce magazine-type documents on a regular basis, or who need to work on the computer with large amounts of text that has been printed or typed.

Resolution

In exactly the same way that the image on a computer screen is made up of dots and the output from a printer is made up of dots, scanners also turn pictures into dots. The main factor in determining the quality of a scanner is its *resolution* or how many dots it can cope with. Just like printers, scanners are measured by the number of dots that they can fit into an inch, or **dpi**. The higher the dpi, the better the final image will be and the better the scanner is. When purchasing a scanner, you should avoid anything much less than 1200 dpi unless you do not mind blocky-looking images.

Handheld scanners

It is also important to consider the size of the things that you will want to scan. There are two types of scanner, *hand-held* and *flatbed*. As the names suggest, hand-held scanners are a bit like portable bar-code readers, except that you need a steady hand. You place the scanner on the document you want to scan and then roll it over the surface to scan the image – in strips if it is wider than your scanner so that you have to re-assemble the picture afterwards.

Flatbed scanners

Flatbeds are more like photocopiers – a flat surface that you place the picture on before closing the lid and doing the scan. You cannot scan something larger than the surface area of a flatbed scanner in one go; instead, you would have to scan it in chunks, and then use a software program for manipulating pictures to line the bits up and connect them together again by hand.

Colour recognition

The degree of colour recognition of a scanner also plays an important part. A small number of specialist machines work only in black and white, with any shade or colour coming out as one of the two in the final image. More commonly, black and white scanners include up to 256 different shades of grey. This will often be referred to as **8-bit** in adverts. Colour scanners are mostly described as **24-bit** or **TrueColour**; either way, that means that the device can recognise up to 17.6 million different colours and shades and incorporate them into the image, giving you a very accurate copy of the document being scanned.

The files that this produces tend to take up a lot of hard disk space, however, so if you expect to be doing a lot of scanning, you should try to make sure that you have a large hard drive. The space taken up by scanned images is easy to underestimate and it can be astonishing just how much space they actually use. A standard five-inch by eight-inch colour photograph can easily use up 1MB on your hard disk.

Optical character recognition

Scanners have a second common usage apart from loading photos into a machine, however, and that is *Optical Character Recognition*, or **OCR** for short. This involves the computer analysing the lines on the pictures sent back by the scanner and looking for patterns that it recognises as letters. In other words, the computer scans the picture for words, and when it finds one, it stores it as plain text.

If you scan and OCR a page of typing, the system should copy the words off the page and onto your computer, ready to be loaded into a word processor or DTP program. The image files that scanners produce are pictures and the computer sees the whole picture as one solid block – they cannot normally be used by a word processor. The text has to be extracted by OCR before it can be manipulated.

Some OCR systems are better than others and they all return results of different quality depending on the typeface of the original print. Few of them can recognise natural handwriting and are only for use with typed or printed text.

OCR text is notorious for being full of misspellings, errors, and sometimes even blank spaces. This is particularly true when trying to obtain text from thin paper as the brightness of the scanning light can cause lines to show through from the other side of the page. Despite these limitations, however, if you need to transfer a lot of typed text from paper into a computer system, scanning and OCR text is going to be far faster and easier than having it all retyped into a word processor by hand.

Twain compatible

'TWAIN compatible' or '*TWAIN compliant*' means that the scanner conforms to a particular standard method of communicating its results to the computer.

Most scanners and scanning devices you can buy these days are TWAIN compatible, but as long as the scanner comes with the necessary software drivers to communicate with your computer, there will not be a problem.

Image file types

There are a wide variety of types of image file, all different ways of storing the picture on the disk, but the most important ones are JPG (or JPEG), GIF, TIFF and bitmap (or BMP). The exact differences between these types are largely irrelevant, but as long as the scanning software can output to one or more of these types of image, you will have no problems using the pictures you scan.

Chapter 6

Dictionary of Technical Terms

This dictionary will help you to understand exactly what it is the personal computer trade is trying to say in its adverts and press releases. Many of the terms in here are not discussed in this book; these are terms that are not of particular concern to someone looking to buy a computer. But they are terms you are likely to come across in advertisements or magazine articles. Although we have tried to cover everything, the computer world is unceasing in its efforts to bury people in jargon and there are bound to be a few things that we missed or that have developed since release. Despite this, there should not be many terms that are not to be found here. A word or phrase in italics in the definition has its own dictionary entry.

10x   Short-hand for 'Ten Times'; means that a given *CD-ROM Drive* is ten times faster than is necessary to play music.

24-Pin   Tells the number of rods in the print head of a *dot matrix printer*. 9-pin dot matrix printers are inferior to 24-pin ones.

286   An obsolete IBM-compatible computer *processor*.

2x   Short-hand for 'Two Times'; means that a given *CD-ROM Drive* is two times faster than is necessary to play music.

32x   Short-hand for 'Thirty-two Times'; means that a given *CD-ROM Drive* is thirty-two times faster than is necessary to play music.

386   An obsolete IBM-compatible computer *processor*.

3D Graphics Card   A type of *graphics card* that has a special inbuilt ability to help process three dimensional graphics quickly and smoothly.

486   An almost obsolete IBM-compatible computer *processor*. The *586* has replaced it.

4x   Short-hand for 'Four Times'; means that a given *CD-ROM Drive* is four times faster than is necessary to play music.

586   The current standard of *processor* used in new IBM-compatible computers.

6x   Short-hand for 'Six Times'; means that a given *CD-ROM Drive* is six times faster than is necessary to play music.

8086   A long-obsolete IBM-compatible computer *processor*.

8x	Short-hand for 'Eight Times'; means that a given CD-ROM Drive is eight times faster than is necessary to play music.
9-Pin	Tells the number of rods in the print head of a *dot matrix printer*. 9-pin dot matrix printers are inferior to 24-pin ones.
ASCII	Abbreviation for American Standard Code for Information Interchange.
Barcoder	A device that attaches to a computer and reads bar codes.
Baud	The rate at which a *modem* transmits information.
Bit	One single unit of information; can either be 0 or 1.
Bitmap	A format used for storing pictures in a computer *file*.
Blurfl	Nonsense word that is used to represent irrelevant text or data.
BMP	Abbreviation for Bitmap; a format used for storing pictures on a computer.
Bus	Part of the internal workings of a *processor* that transmits information from one area of the computer to another.
Byte	Eight bits; the amount of information needed to identify a *character*.
Cache	An area of *memory* that holds information ready for when the *processor* wants it so as to speed things up.
CD	Abbreviation for Compact Disc.
CDR/CDRW Disk Drive	Compact Disc Write/Compact Disk Read/Re-Write.
CD-ROM	Compact Disc Read-Only Memory; a *CD* that has computer information stored on it.
CD-ROM Drive	A device that allows the computer to read the information from a *CD-ROM*.
Character	One letter, number, space or typographic symbol.
Chatting	The *Internet* practice of typing messages to other people that are received and replied to in real time, without any delay.
Chip	Silicon-based electronics that can perform calculations and store data.
CPU	Central processing unit.
Database	A *program* that stores information and can search through it to find those pieces that match certain specifications.
Desktop	The type of computer that has to be set up on a working surface and connected to a mains power supply before it can be used.

Disk	A type of device that can be used to store computer information on a permanent or semi-permanent basis.
Docking Station	A device to which a portable computer can be connected so that it can be used like a desktop computer.
DOS	The standard text-based user interface of IBM-compatible machines.
Dot Matrix	A type of *printer*.
Daisywheel	A type of *printer*.
DPI	Dots Per Inch; a measure of *resolution*.
DRAM	An old type of *RAM* chip.
Drive	A device that can read (and often write) information from or to a *disk*.
Driver	A *program* that operates a *peripheral* for the user.
DTP	DeskTop Publishing; the process of designing and laying out documents that includes graphical elements.
DV	A new, standard type of *CD-ROM*.
EDO	A type of *RAM* chip.
EGA	A now-obsolete standard for computer *monitor* displays.
EIDE	Enhanced *IDE*; a standard type of *hard disk*.
Email	Electronic Mail.
Explorer	Short for Internet Explorer; a commercial product used to view the Internet's *World-Wide Web*.
Fanfold	A type of *printer* paper where the sheets are connected at top and bottom and have rows of perforated holes attached to either side.
FD	A *floppy disk* or a *floppy drive*.
FDD	*Floppy disk drive*.
File	A collection of related pieces of information stored as one unit on a *disk*.
Floppy	A type of portable disk that holds a modest amount of information.
Floppy Drive	The device that allows the computer to read from and write to a *floppy disk*.
FTP	File Transfer Protocol; the *Internet* tool that allows users to copy *files* from distant machines.
GB	*Gigabyte*, or 1,000,000,000 *bytes*.

Gfx	Abbreviation for the word 'graphics'.
GIF	A format used for storing pictures in a computer file.
Gigabyte	1,000,000,000 *bytes*.
Graphics	A bit of equipment that speeds up the *processor* by doing all the Card calculations involving images.
Handshaking	The technique that two *modems* use to negotiate the speeds and *protocols* that they will use to communicate.
Hard Disk	A type of non-portable *disk* that stores large amounts of information. Also known as a *hard drive* or a *hard disk drive*.
Hardware	The physical devices and other bits of equipment that are used in a computer system, as opposed to the *software*, or *programs*.
Hayes	Indicates that a modem can communicate using the Hayes standards compatible for *handshaking*.
HD	*Hard Disk*.
HDD	*Hard Disk Drive*.
HTML	The language used to write pages for display on the *World-Wide Web*.
IDE	An older standard type of *Hard Drive*.
Image	A picture or other type of data that is presented visually.
Inkjet	A type of *printer*.
Integrated	General term meaning 'all linked together into one unit'.
Interface	A connector, generally at the back of a machine, that allows a computer to be connected to some other device.
Internet	A global *network* of computers that share information and *email*.
Intranet	A *network* of computers that all belong to one organisation.
IRC	Internet Relay Chat; the Internet tool that allows people to type messages back and forth to each other in real time.
ISA	A standard type of *bus*.
ISDN	A high-speed telephone line suitable for large volumes of data.
ISP	Internet Service Provider; a company which sells *Internet* access.
Java	The language used to write animated pictures and other advanced things for display on the *World-Wide Web*.

JPEG	A format used for storing pictures in a computer file.
JPG	A format used for storing pictures in a computer file.
KB	*Kilobytes*, or 1000 *bytes*.
KBPS	*Kilobytes* per second; the measurement of *Baud*, or *modem* speed.
Keyboard	The typewriter-like device used to enter letters, numbers and typographic symbols into a computer.
Kilobyte	1000 *bytes*.
LAN	*Local Area Network* or a *network* that only links computers that are physically close.
Laptop	A large, somewhat obsolete type of *portable* computer.
Laser	A type of *printer*.
LCD	Liquid Crystal Display.
Local Area Network	A *network* that links computers that are physically close.
Mac	The Apple Macintosh; a range of personal computers that are not IBM-compatible, but are instead direct competitors.
MB	*Megabyte*, or 1,000,000 *bytes*.
Megabyte	1,000,000 *bytes*.
MegaHertz	1,000,000 cycles per second.
Memory	The storage space used by computers to hold information.
MHz	*MegaHertz*.
Modem	Device that allows a computer to talk to another computer via a telephone connection.
Monitor	Screen that allows a computer to display information visually.
Mouse	Device used to move an image of a pointer around on a computer *monitor*, so as to give instructions to a *program*.
MPEG	Format used for storing movie clips in a computer file.
MPG	Format used for storing movie clips in a computer file.
MUD	*Multi-User Dimension*, an *Internet* game that is played by several people simultaneously and involves creating the illusion of a separate reality.

MUG	*Multi-User Game*, an *Internet* game that is played by several people simultaneously and involves creating the illusion of a separate reality.
Netscape	A popular commercial piece of software used to view the *World-Wide Web*.
Network	Two or more computers linked together so that they can send information to each other.
News	The *Internet* tool that allows messages grouped by general topic to be transmitted world-wide.
NLQ	Near Letter Quality: says that the output from a *printer* looks almost, but not quite, as good as if typewritten.
Non-Interlaced	A standard way for a computer *monitor* to build up an image.
Notebook	A type of *portable* computer.
OCR (Optical Character Recognition)	The process that allows the letters represented inside a computer *image* file to be converted into computer text.
P75	A type of *Pentium* processor that works at 75 *MHz*.
P120	A type of *Pentium* processor that works at 120 *MHz*.
P133	A type of *Pentium* processor that works at 133 *MHz*.
P150	A type of *Pentium* processor that works at 150 *MHz*.
P166	A type of *Pentium* processor that works at 166 *MHz*.
P200	A type of *Pentium* processor that works at 200 *MHz*.
P400	A type of *Pentium* processor that works at 400 *MHz*.
Palette	The range of colours available at any one time for use with an *image*.
Palmtop	A very small *portable* computer.
Parallel	A type of computer interface.
PC	Personal Computer, specifically one which is IBM compatible.
PC Card	A type of *interface*. Previously known as *PCMCIA*.
Pci	A standard type of *bus*.
PCMCIA	A type of *interface* often used in *portable* computers.
Pentium	The current standard of IBM-compatible *processor*.
Peripheral	A device that connects to a computer.

Pipeline Burst Cache   A type of *cache* recommended for *Pentium* machines.

Plotter   A type of *printer*.

Plug & Play   A type of *interface* that theoretically allows an expansion to be simply fitted into place and be ready for use.

Port   Any connector between the computer and an external device.

Portable   A computer that can be operated by battery and used whilst travelling or away from a standard electrical mains supply.

Powerbook   A type of *portable* computer.

PPM   Pages Per Minute; a measurement of the speed of a *printer*.

PPP   A standard form of communication *protocol* used for talking to the *Internet*.

Printer   A device that transfers output from a computer onto paper.

Processor   The main brain of a computer.

Program   A set of instructions that tell a computer exactly what to do.

Protocol   A set of conventions used when transmitting data between two *modems*.

RAM   Random Access Memory; a type of information storage space.

Refresh Rate   The speed at which a *monitor* re-draws the screen.

Resolution   The number of dots that a computer device squeezes into a specific area.

Rollerball   A small ball used to replace a *mouse* on some portable computers.

ROM   Read Only Memory; a type of *memory* where vital computer instructions and *programs* are stored.

RX   Contraction of 'Receive'; one of the lights on an *external modem*.

Scanner   A device that reads a picture or other *image* into a computer.

SCSI   A fast type of *hard disk*.

SDRAM   A type of *memory* used on *Graphics Cards*.

Serial   A type of computer *interface*.

Sim   A type of *RAM* chip.

SLIP   A standard form of communication *protocol* used for talking to the *Internet*.

Software   The non-physical parts of a computer system; the *programs*.

Spreadsheet	A type of *program* used for analysing numerical data.
Static RAM	A type of *RAM* chip that is not blanked when it loses power.
SVGA	A standard for computer *monitor* displays.
Syquest	A type of portable *hard disk*.
Talkware	An *Internet* tool for transmitting speech across the network in real time.
Targa	A format used for storing pictures in a computer file.
TCP/IP	A standard form of communication *protocol* used for talking to the *Internet*.
Telnet	An *Internet* tool for logging onto a distant machine.
TGA	*Targa*; a format used for storing pictures in a computer file.
Thermal	An obsolete type of printer.
TIFF	A format used for storing pictures in a computer file.
Toner	The powdered ink used by *laser printers*.
Tower	A type of *DeskTop* computer.
Trackerball	A device sometimes used to replace a *mouse* on a *portable* computer.
TrueColor	A standard for working with high-quality computer *images*.
TWAIN	A standard communication method for *scanners*.
TX	'Transmit'; one of the lights on the front of an *external modem*.
Usenet News	An *Internet* tool that allows messages grouped by general topic to be transmitted worldwide.
V32	A standard *modem* communication *protocol* for speeds up to 14.4Kbps.
V34	A standard *modem* communication *protocol* for speeds up to 28.8Kbps.
V34 Plus	A standard *modem* communication *protocol* for speeds up to 33.6Kbps.
V90	A standard *modem* communication *protocol* for speeds up to 56.5Kbps.
VESA	A standard type of *bus*.
VGA	A standard for computer *monitor* displays.
VL	A standard type of *bus*.
VT100	A near-obsolete standard for computer *monitor* displays kept alive by certain *Internet* requirements.

VT102   A near-obsolete standard for computer *monitor* displays kept alive by certain *Internet* requirements.

WAN   *Wide Area Network*; a *network* in which the machines are a long distance part.

Wax   An obsolete type of *printer*.

**Wide Area
Network**   A *network* in which the machines are a long distance apart.

Windows   The standard graphical user interface of IBM-compatible machines.

**Word
Processor**   A program that allows text to be manipulated.

**World-Wide
Web**   The *Internet* tool that allows magazine-like pages of text, images and sometimes sounds and movie clips to be viewed.

WRAM   A standard type of *memory* used in *graphics cards*.

WWW   *World-Wide Web*.

Part Two
How To Use Your Computer

Chapter 7

Your Workstation

For the absolute beginner the thought of using a computer can be a nightmare. However, simply knowing a few facts can quickly dissolve this illusion. Look at it this way – most households have a range of electrical products. Be it a music centre, Hi-Fi system or a CD player. Most have one or two television sets and the accompanying video player. Then there is the washing machine, the tumble dryer and the microwave oven. There are also the complicated machinations of setting the clock-timer on the electric cooker, which most adults find easy to program.

If you can operate (*program*) any of these products then you will have no trouble in learning to use a modern day computer. You will find that the computer is just as robust as any other household appliance as long as you treat it with the same respect.

Before you begin using your computer you will need some space to place the various components: a decent sized work-desk to place the monitor and keyboard; a nearby space to place the computer itself. The computer will have to be placed close by the monitor as the length of the electrical connections regulates this distance. If you have a printer it will also have to be placed at least within one to two metres of the computer due to the connections. Most computer superstores now sell workstations that are adequate for most needs.

Once the computer equipment workstation is set up you will need a comfortable seat. The best ergo-dynamical position to sit is with your back upright and your elbows bent and tucked into your waist with your wrists horizontal to the desk surface. This will help to reduce fatigue when sitting at your computer for long periods.

Diag 1 – Workstation

The Keyboard – This enables you to communicate with the computer. Anything that you type will be displayed on the monitor. Only when you press the *return key*, that's the largest key with the arrow marked on it, will the information be processed by the computer and in certain modes an answer displayed on the monitor. If the computer doesn't respond to a keypress immediately, don't panic and keep pressing the keypad. Wait a while for the computer to process the information you have input. Far more frustration and mistakes are generated by not being patient, resulting in the computer processing incorrect information.

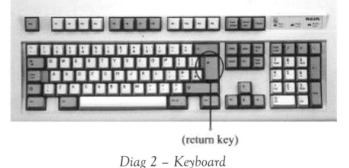

(return key)

Diag 2 – Keyboard

The Mouse – This is a pointing device that is supplementary to the keyboard. As you move your mouse on a flat surface, a pointer moves on your screen, enabling you to place the cursor where you wish to type or click. To point, move the mouse until the tip of the pointer on the screen is over the item or area you want to point to. It works on the principle that when you place the mouse pointer on an icon or menu on your screen and then depress the mouse button (click), an action will be performed on that item. This is explained more fully in the text on word processors and other programs later.

Diag 3 – Mouse

The Monitor – The function of the monitor is to give you a visual display. When you depress keys on your keyboard, it will display the letters that you have depressed. It will also display a menu and icons that have been visually produced by the program that you are using. Warning messages will sometimes appear automatically on your screen. The program you are using produces these messages to help you complete the task in hand.

Diag 4 – Monitor

The Printer – This is a device for transferring the electronic information stored in your computer to hard copy on paper. If you want to use your computer for writing letters, reports etc., then a printer is essential. Most people need to be able to print out information from their computer, whether it be for business or pleasure. Many people prefer to have a hard copy of important documents, and some like to print out the emails they have received, rather than just reading them on screen.

Diag 5 – Printer

Chapter 8

Navigating Windows

In 1981 IBM marketed its first personal computer, and Microsoft released **MS-DOS** (*Microsoft Disk Operating System*). The **PC** or *Personal Computer* revolution had begun.

It was inevitable that a certain amount of training would be necessary for operators to understand how to use these machines. For when you pressed the *'power on'* button on your computer, the machine would *boot up* and you would be greeted by a blank monitor sporting the characters **C:** in the top left-hand corner of the screen. For the untrained user, if you were not precise when inputting instructions to get your program running, nothing would happen, and you would be left staring at a blank screen.

Windows 3.0

It was during the 1980s that Microsoft introduced their first versions of Windows, but it was in 1990, that Microsoft introduced Windows 3.0. This version was a tremendous breakthrough, for now users were really able to maximise productivity. Windows 3.0 made computers easier to use, application easier to run, and allowed several applications to run at the same time. But to use this version of Windows it was necessary to have a hard-disk in your machine with a minimum of about 8 to 10MB of storage, which at the time was very expensive.

To get the Windows program to work you would have to input the instruction:
C:\windows\win. Then you would have to press the **return key** for the computer to respond by opening the Windows program. Another way of making Windows open automatically was to place an instruction in the **'Autoexec.bat'** file, which

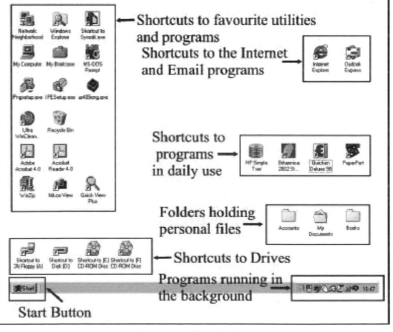

Diag 6 – The Desktop

is run by the *Disk Operating System* upon boot-up.

Nowadays everything has changed. When the start button is depressed the computer comes to life and automatically the **'Windows'** program takes over where the **'DOS'** program stops. Inputting instructions is now outdated. **'Icons'** shown on what is called your **'Desktop'** now represent those instructions. Here you will find the start button and taskbar at the bottom of your screen when you start Windows for the first time. All this has come about with the design of Windows 95, and the later versions of Windows 98, Windows *Me* and Windows^{xp}.

Windows 95/98

Windows 95 was a big leap forward in windows technology when it took over from Windows 3.1. It did, however, need a lot more memory and hard disk space to operate. Three years later, as manufacturers built faster machines and memory became cheaper, new machines were sold already loaded with Windows 98, bringing the end user a more stable operating system and a few extra programs thrown in. For those who still use the older, slower computers, Windows 95 and 98 are widely used. Only those who have remained faithful to their vintage machines, which by now are very limited in their use, are still using Windows 3.1.

Windows Millennium Edition

Windows *Me* includes many new features. Your computer will start more quickly, and there is added protection to prevent important work from being lost. These improvements make Windows more reliable, and as expected with any software upgrade, Windows *Me* gives many improvements over its predecessors.

For a start, the desktop looks different, but it is mostly cosmetic. Most importantly is the way in which it recognises new hardware. You only need to change your printer or scanner and immediately the **'Plug and Play'** program comes into operation. When the installation is complete the new equipment will work instantly, without rebooting the system.

Windows Movie Maker will go down a treat for those who are interested in making their own videos. With this *add-on* software you can edit your own video sequences from sources such as camcorders or digital cameras. You can create films, save images of important events, or enable distance learning. You can even create a slide show using your own digital pictures or pictures you import to your computer.

'Hibernate' is an excellent new feature that can save a lot of frustration when the computer is accidentally turned off, or when you are called away for an hour or so, and don't want to close the file you are working on. Provided the Hibernate feature is turned on, you can safely turn-off the computer without closing your files, and find when it is switched back on, any files that were left open, and unsaved, will be there on your screen for you to continue working.

Windows *Me* also protects important system files by using **'System File Protection'**. System File Protection works in the background, so you will probably be unaware that it is there. It is, however, an important piece of software and can save you a lot of headaches when new software is installed.

Whenever you install a new program on your hard drive, many new files are added to your system files where they are shared by other programs. Sometimes these files may pre-date the ones already installed and overwrite the newer versions. Consequently other programs using the same file will cease to work properly. To make sure such things don't happen, System File Protection prevents the newer files from being overwritten, and this ensures that your copy of Windows, and your favourite programs, operate smoothly and quickly.

Windows^{xp}

Windows^{xp} is now the latest version to be pre-installed by manufacturers of new machines. However, if you want to upgrade from the previous Windows version, it is as well to understand that this latest version will only work on machines that have a minimum 233MHz processor or faster, and 128MB or more of RAM. You will also need a hard disk with at least 1.5GB of free space available. In addition, there are certain other features (that we do not need to go into here), within Windows^{xp} that require additional hardware.

When you boot up the first thing that you will notice is the new user interface. A welcome screen tutorial sets up and configures your personal details, including your Internet settings. It then registers the product with Microsoft via your modem.

Windows^{xp} has a completely new feel compared with all earlier versions of Windows. Familiar features have undergone a complete visual overhaul. At first glance, colours look much brighter and deeper. The shapes of buttons and tags are more rounded than in previous versions. The Start Menu and the Control Panel show group categories, such as **'My Pictures'** or **'My Music'**.

The Welcome screen is the first thing you encounter and is the place where user names are shown that can include a photo of the individual. Passwords aren't necessary, but can be used if required. Fast switching between users is a breeze. If a new user wants to access their files there is no need to log off, or close the applications that are running. All your data and settings will remain as you have left them. The new user simply *logs on* and starts working in their own environment.

What was once the recently used 'document' drop down list, accessed from the start button is now a desktop feature. Recently used files remain visible as icons, on the desktop, while folders that aren't accessed regularly are dropped from view, thus ridding the *Start* menu of clutter.

In conclusion

The environments provided by Windows, regardless of the version you are running, are not overall dissimilar. Each version provides an efficient way of working with the programs on your computer. And as each version is improved, so you get more and more add-on software to help you run your computer faster and more efficiently than ever before.

Therefore, it makes no difference what version of Windows you use, your third-party programs will not work any differently from how they are supposed to work. If you haven't got exactly the same programs as the ones described in this book, don't worry. Most programs of the same type, regardless of whether they run under Windows or not, i.e. wordprocessing programs, number crunchers, or graphic design programs, will all offer matching facilities and function in a similar way.

Folders and shortcuts to programs

When you first look at your computer desktop it can be quite confusing. Unfamiliar icons stare back, daring you to touch them with the mouse pointer. Happily this situation can very quickly and easily be sorted out.

Use the analogy that what you see on the computer screen is equivalent to looking at the surface of your desk worktop. Each icon represents a folder that contains information to the whereabouts of a computer program or file. If each icon had material properties you would have to physically open the folder to see what's inside, then you would have to physically retrieve the program or file from its location.

In an electronic environment all that is physically required is to move the mouse pointer over the icon on your desktop screen and depress the left mouse button; once to select the icon, (you will know the icon is selected because it will be highlighted) then twice more in quick succession to open the folder and execute the instructions. Within seconds the file will be on the screen in front of you.

Creating a new folder

The desktop is a very handy place to keep 'often used' files that you have created. As an exercise, we are going to create our own personal folder on the desktop. We will call the folder **'Personal Letters'**.

- Place the mouse cursor over a blank area of your desktop screen.

- Click the right mouse button once. A drop-down menu will appear.

- Place the mouse cursor over **'New'** – a further drop-down menu will appear.

- Place the mouse cursor over **'Folder'** and click the left mouse button once. The drop-down menu will disappear and an icon representing a folder will appear with the words **'New Folder'** blinking in a small box beneath.

- Type the title **'Personal Letters'** to replace the words in the box.

- Press the **'return'** key.

That's all there is to it. To open the folder, place the mouse pointer over the folder, press the left mouse button to select, then double click the left mouse button to open the folder. If you so wish you can create another folder inside the folder you have just created.

Creating shortcuts to programs on the desktop

Although the initial stages of creating a shortcut is easy, completing the task can be difficult. In fact, for the novice who has never before used a computer it is virtually impossible. However, after saying that, the following steps will guide you through the task of setting up a desktop shortcut to your **'Windows Explorer'** program, thus making your desktop a more versatile environment to work in.

☐ Place the mouse pointer over a blank area of your desktop screen. Click the right mouse button once. A drop-down menu will appear.

☐ Place the mouse pointer over **'New'** in the drop-down menu, and a further drop-down menu will appear.

☐ Place the mouse pointer over **'Shortcut'** in the new drop-down menu, then click the left mouse button once. The drop-down menu will disappear and a window titled **'Create Shortcut'** will appear.

☐ Place the mouse pointer over **'Browse'** and click the left mouse button once. A window titled **'Browse'** will appear.

☐ Locate the horizontal cursor in the browse window and move it by holding down the left mouse button and dragging it to the right. (It looks like a grey bar with black arrow heads at each end.) Release the mouse button when you see the folder named **'Windows'**.

☐ Place the mouse pointer over the folder **'Windows'** and double click the left mouse button. The **'Windows'** folder will open revealing more folders.

☐ Once again locate the horizontal cursor in the browse window and move it by holding down the left mouse button and dragging it to the right. Release the mouse button when you see the file named **'Explorer'**.

☐ Highlight the **'Explorer'** icon, (not the words) with one click of the left mouse button, then double click the left mouse button.

☐ The **'Browse'** window will close and the **'Create Shortcut'** window will become active. Look in the command window and you will see the path to the Windows Explorer program printed for you.

☐ Move the mouse pointer to the button titled **'Next'**. Click the left mouse button once. The **'Browse'** window will close and a further window titled **'Select a Title for the Program'** will open. In the box under the words **'Select a name for the shortcut'** will be the title **'Explorer'** already typed for you.

☐ Move the mouse pointer to the button titled **'Finish'**. Click the left mouse button once. The window will close and an icon will appear on your desktop with the title **'Explorer'** underneath.

Test the shortcut by moving your mouse pointer to the icon. Click the left mouse button once to select, then double click the left mouse button to open the program. When you are satisfied that the shortcut works to your satisfaction close the program.

When you become conversant with the names and types of icons used by different programs (of which there are thousands), you will find it quite easy to make your own shortcuts to your favourite programs.

Creating shortcuts to programs on the start menu

This is the same 'Create Shortcut' window that you accessed when you created your shortcut to 'Explorer'. The only difference is that when the shortcut is created it will appear on your 'Start Menu' and not on your desktop. This is an extremely good place to create shortcuts as it prevents the desktop from becoming cluttered up with too many icons.

- Place the mouse pointer at the bottom of your screen on 'Start'. Click the left mouse button once on 'Start' to open the menu.

- Move the mouse pointer to 'Settings', a further menu will appear, then click the left mouse button on 'Taskbar & Start Menu'. A window titled 'Taskbar Properties' will open.

- Select the tab titled 'Start Menu Programs'. Select the button titled 'Add' with your left mouse button. The window 'Create Shortcut' will appear.

- Place the mouse pointer over 'Browse' and click the left mouse button once. A window titled 'Browse' will appear.

- Locate the horizontal cursor in the browse window and move it by holding down the left mouse button and dragging it to the right. (It looks like a grey bar with black arrow heads at each end.) Release the mouse button when you see the folder named 'Windows'.

- Place the mouse pointer over the folder 'Windows' and double click the left mouse button. The 'Windows' folder will open revealing more folders.

- Once again locate the horizontal cursor in the browse window and move it by holding down the left mouse button and dragging it to the right. Release the mouse button when you see the file named 'Explorer'.

- Highlight the 'Explorer' icon, (not the words) with one click of the left mouse button, then double click the left mouse button.

- The 'Browse' window will close and the 'Create Shortcut' window will become active. Look in the command window and you will see the path to the windows Explorer program printed for you.

□ Move the mouse pointer to the button titled **'Next'**. Click the left mouse button once. The **'Browse'** window will close and a further window titled **'Select a Title for the Program'** will open. In the box under the words **'Select a name for the shortcut'** will be the title **'Explorer'** already typed for you.

□ Move the mouse pointer to the button titled **'Finish'**. Click the left mouse button once. The window will close and the shortcut to **'Explorer'** will be included on your start menu.

□ Move the mouse pointer to **'OK'**. Click the left mouse button once and the window will close.

□ Test the shortcut by moving your mouse pointer over **'Start'**. Click the left mouse button once to open the drop down list, then click the left mouse button on **'Programs'** to see the drop down list of programs.

□ Mover the mouse pointer over the title **'Explorer'** and click once with the left mouse button. The Explorer program will open.

Starting a program from the run command

The **'Run'** command is yet another method of opening a program. If you are not sure where the program is or how to specify the path you can often specify just the name of the program instead.

□ Use the left mouse button to click on the **'Start'** button and then again on **'Run'**.

□ Type the name of the program in the window provided e.g. **'Wordpad'** then click the left mouse button on the **'OK'** tab.

Keyboard shortcuts whilst viewing the desktop

Although **Microsoft Windows** is very easily operated by the mouse, you can use keyboard shortcuts to carry out most of the tasks. Here is a short selection of the most regularly used shortcuts that are available before selecting an item on your desktop.

□ To see the Help menu – press **F1**.

□ To toggle the start menu on and off – press **ALT+TAB**.

□ To find a file or folder – press **F3**. The Find a File or Folder will appear. Type the name of the item you want to find and the computer will give you a list of files or folders that include the words that you have typed.

□ To open the Start menu – press **ALT+S**.

□ To close down or reboot – press **ALT+F4**.

□ To display the Start menu – press **CTRL+ESC**.

□ To bypass AutoPlay when inserting a compact disc – press **SHIFT** while inserting the CD-ROM.

□ To change the properties of your desktop – press **SHIFT+F10.** A menu will appear giving you the option of changing the Desktop properties, altering the time on the task bar and enabling a new Tools bar to be designed.

□ To delete a folder or file on the desktop – highlight the item and press **DELETE**

□ To delete a file immediately without placing the file in the Recycle Bin press **SHIFT+DEL**

□ To rename a folder – highlight the icon, press **F2**. Just type a new name in the box below the icon and press return.

□ To view the properties of a file press **ALT+ENTER** or **ALT + double-click the left mouse button**

□ To copy a file to another location – press **CONTROL** while dragging the file to its new location

□ To create a shortcut to a file or program – press **CTRL+SHIFT** while dragging the file to its new location

□ To copy a file to another location – press **CTRL+C** then place the mouse pointer in the new location and press **CTRL+V**. This is known as copying and pasting.

□ To move an item from one location to another location – press **CTRL+X** then place the mouse pointer in the new location and press **CTRL+V**. This is known as cutting and pasting.

□ To view the shortcut menu for a selected item – press **SHIFT+F10**

To move the mouse pointer by using MouseKeys

Microsoft have included software in Windows to enable the mouse pointer to be moved utilising the numeric pad. To move the pointer horizontally or vertically, press the 'Up', 'Down', 'Left' and 'Right' arrow keys. To move the pointer diagonally, press 'Home', 'End', 'Page Up', and 'Page down' keys. Follow these instructions to activate this option:

□ On the desktop use the **'Tab'** button to highlight **'Start'** then press **'Return'**.

□ Use the up arrow key to move the highlighted selection to **'Settings'**.

□ Use the right arrow key to select **'Control Panel'**. Now press **'Return'**. The 'Control Panel' will open.

☐ Use the down arrow key to select the icon entitled **'Accessibility Options'**. (It should be the first icon in the list.) Press **'Return'** and you will see various options to change the mouse settings.

☐ Hold down the **'Control'** key and at the same time keep depressing the **'tab'** key until the tab titled **'Mouse'** is highlighted, then press **'Return'**. This action will open a window showing a small box titled **'MouseKeys'**.

☐ Keep depressing the 'Tab' key until the blank square to the left of the words **'MouseKeys'** is highlighted, then press **'Return'**.

☐ Keep depressing the 'Tab' key until **'Apply'** is highlighted, then press **'Return'**.

☐ Keep depressing the 'Tab' key until **'OK'** is highlighted, then press **'Return'**.

☐ Close the **'Control Panel'** by depressing the **'Escape'** key.

After rebooting the computer, you will be able to use the numeric keypad arrow keys to move the mouse pointer. When the pointer is in the desired location, press the centre numeric key (5) to select, then depress 'Return'. (The effect of 'MouseKeys' will not always work until you have rebooted the computer.)

Alternatively:

☐ Press the **'Left Alt button'**+**'Left Shift button'** and the **'Num Lock'** button simultaneously. You will find the **'Num Lock'** button situated at the top left of your numeric keypad.

This action will enable you to move the mouse pointer using the arrow keys on your numeric keypad.

Note: To use the numbers pad to enter numbers you will have to press the **'Left Alt button'**+**'Left Shift button'** and the **'Num Lock'** simultaneously to cancel this action.

BASIC WORDPROCESSING

OK, let's get started. Switch on your computer and wait for the Windows 'Desktop' to appear on your screen. You will hear the hard-disk whirring and probably a red light flickering on your console. Some computers have the letters H.D.D. written close to the red light. The 'boot-up', as it is called, will take between thirty seconds and one minute.

The Start button on the desktop will always be visible when Windows is running. This will remain so until such time as you wish to change it. When you place the mouse pointer on the **'Start button'** and click the left mouse button once, the **'Start'** menu opens to let you see the list of programs installed on your computer.

All programs open in a similar way, and as an exercise we will open the program called **'Wordpad'** as this is part of the **'Windows'** package. Begin as follows:

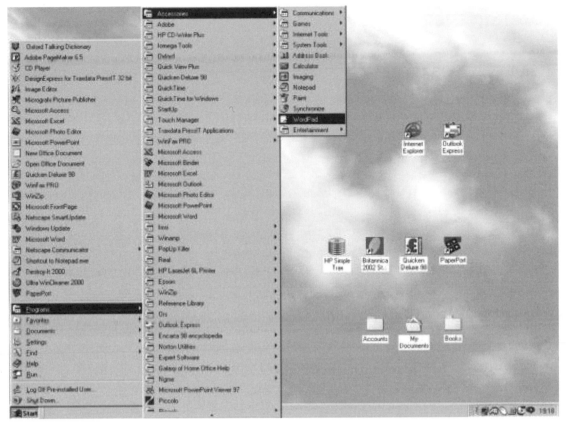

Diag 7 - The Start Menu

☐ Place the mouse pointer over **'Start'** and click the left mouse button. A menu will appear.

☐ Place the mouse pointer over **'Programs'** and click the left mouse button, a further drop-down menu will appear.

☐ Place the mouse pointer over **'Accessories'** and click the left mouse button, a further drop-down menu will appear.

☐ Place the mouse pointer over **'Wordpad'** click the left mouse button and the word processor program **'Wordpad'** will open. A blank document will appear on the screen.

Creating text

Little notice is taken of the difficulties a beginner has when trying to find the way around the computer keyboard whilst typing text. Considering that the keyboard is the main method of communicating with the computer's processor, this is a serious oversight. Unfortunately, program makers use specialised keys, or combinations of keys for different commands making it difficult for a comprehensive overview for instruction. That being the case, I will attempt to explain in general terms how to use the keyboard to the best advantage when using any of the most well-known wordprocessing programs.

Positioning the cursor

Here is an exercise to help you learn to position the cursor accurately. Type the following line of text, complete with the deliberate spelling error:

- 'It is not easy to write about the nine years of day and night driving on <u>hte</u> streets in and around Berlin. There was drama: I did not hurt anyone, I did not smash any cars or other things and kept a clean licence.'

- Move the cursor with the mouse, (it is indicated by an **I** beam) so that it is positioned in front of the misspelt word, then click the left mouse button once. The cursor will remain in place. Here is the text again with the cursor shown in place as an **I** beam.

- 'It is not easy to write about the nine years of day and night driving on **I**<u>hte</u> streets in and around Berlin. There was drama: I did not hurt anyone, I did not smash any cars or other things and kept a clean licence.

- It is now possible to delete the incorrectly spelt word by pressing the forward delete key, marked with the word **'Delete'**. Gently but firmly, depress the forward delete key to delete one letter at a time. Make sure that you don't hold the forward delete key down, if you do then too much text will be deleted, and you will have to retype more text than is necessary.

- Another way of deleting a character is to place the cursor after it and press the backspace key.

A second way of moving the cursor without using the mouse is to use the 'Arrow Keys' on your keyboard. You will find them on the bottom row of the keyboard; between the **'Ctrl'** key and the **'0'** or **'Ins'** key on the numbers pad.

By using the **'Arrow keys'**, the cursor can be moved anywhere within your document. Once again, it is a case of placing the cursor before or after the words or letters that need alteration.

Removing unwanted spaces is done in the same way as correcting text. Place the cursor before or after the unwanted space(s) and press the delete or backspace key.

The shift keys

The two shift keys are located on the fourth row of keys from top, and are marked with an arrow, thus:

These two keys are used to change from lower to upper case characters. For a shift key to function it has to be held down whilst pressing a letter, digit or punctuation key.

Each punctuation key is marked with two symbols, one above the other. When holding down the 'Shift' key the punctuation symbol at the top of the key can be typed and will be shown on the screen:

_ + { } : @ ~ < > ?

The same rule applies for the digit keys on the top row. When the shift key is held down, the symbols shown above the digits can be typed and will be shown on the screen:

! " £ $ % ^ & * ( )

The tab key

Used in wordprocessing programs for tabulating text. Each time the **'Tab'** key is depressed the cursor will move approximately half an inch to the right. If text has been placed after the cursor, then the text will also be moved to the right. Clicking once with the left mouse button on **'Format'**, which you will find on the menu bar, and then **'Tabs'** on the drop down menu can alter the distance.

The caps lock key

This key is used solely for text. If you want to type using uppercase characters for any length of time, press the **'Caps Lock'** key. When you want to resume typing in lower case, press the **'Caps Lock'** key again. Remember that this key has no other purpose.

Specialised keys

All other keys on the keyboard are peculiar to the computer, and have different functions depending on the program you are using.

The Menu bar in Wordpad: creating a professional look to your document

You have seen how easy it is to create a simple text document. Now you are ready to make the page and text look more like a professional document.

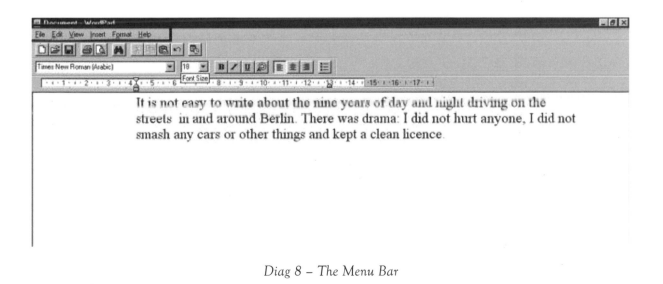

Diag 8 – The Menu Bar

- **To change the font type, style, and size** – Once you have started typing you may want to change the way the text appears. Highlight the text you want to alter by depressing the left mouse button and dragging the pointer over the chosen text. Click the left mouse button on '**Format**', then click the left mouse button on '**Font**'. The '**Font**' drop down menu will appear. Use the left mouse button to select the options you want. You can also specify the font for new text by changing the font settings before you begin to type.

- Before clicking the Format menu you can change the look of your text for an entire document. Click the left mouse button on '**Edit**', and then click the left mouse button on '**Select All**'.

- **Bold; Italics; Underline** – These are three important ways of making parts of your document stand out from the rest. Take a look at the icons beneath the Menu bar. You will see three icons: **B** – bold, *I* – Italics, U – Underline. Highlight the text to be altered by depressing the left mouse button and dragging the pointer over the chosen text. Release the button and move it to the icon of your choice. Click the left mouse button once only on the icon. The highlighted text will now change to its new format.

- **To format a paragraph** – Highlight the paragraph to be altered by depressing the left mouse button and dragging the pointer over the chosen text. Click the left mouse button on '**Format**', then click the left mouse button on '**Paragraph**'. The '**Paragraph**' drop down menu appears. Enter the new values in the windows provided.

- **To personalise the page** – Click the left mouse button on '**File**'. On the drop down menu click the left mouse button on '**Page Setup**': the '**Page Setup**' drop down menu appears. Enter the new values in the windows provided.

- **To set tab stops** – Click the left mouse button on the ruler at each increment where you want a tab stop. To delete tab stops on the ruler, click and hold down the left mouse button on the tab(s) to be removed and drag them off the ruler.

- **Text Wrap** – To alter the way text wraps on your screen click the left mouse button on '**View**', click the left mouse button on '**Options**'. The '**Options**' drop down menu will appear. Click once with the left mouse button on the '**Text**' tab, then select one of three options. '**No wrap**' – '**Wrap to window**' – '**Wrap to ruler**'.

To save and print a file

- Move the mouse pointer to highlight '**File**' on the menu bar. Left mouse click on '**File**'. A drop down menu will appear.

- Move the mouse pointer to highlight '**Save**'. Left mouse click on '**Save**'.

A window will open in the centre of the screen. This is the '**Save Window**'.

- Type a name for the file e.g. '**Test**' in the File Name box then click the left mouse button on the box labelled '**Save**'.

Diag 9 – The Drop Down menu

Printing a file

Make sure there is paper in your printer and that the printer is turned on.

- Move the mouse pointer over the menu bar and using the left mouse button, click on **'File'**. A drop down menu will appear.

- Move the mouse pointer to **'Print'**. Using the left mouse button, click on **'Print'**.

- A window will open in the centre of the screen; this is the **'Print Menu'**.

Diag 9a – The Drop Down menu

Diag 10 – The Print menu

☐ Move the mouse pointer to the box labelled **'OK'** and using the left mouse button, click **'OK'**.

☐ Now turn your attention to the printer where your file will be printed.

You will find that the procedures given for saving and printing files is the same in almost all wordprocessing programs. Other commands on the 'Menu bar' such as: **'New'**, **'Save as'**, **'Document Setup'**, **'Setup Printer'** all work in the same way as you have been shown.

The icons shown below the 'Menu bar' can be used as alternatives. They are in addition to the **'Menu bar'** and are used as shortcuts to the drop down menu commands.

ALWAYS read your screen. Whenever you use the 'Menu bar' an explanation of its function is nearly always displayed, either at the top or bottom of the screen.

Closing a program

To close 'Wordpad' place the mouse pointer over the 'X' in the top right-hand corner and click the left mouse button.

If you have followed these directions to the letter you will have successfully opened and closed a program using the Windows interface. In this case, the program opened was 'Wordpad', a word processing program. In the same way, it is possible to open and close any program running under Windows.

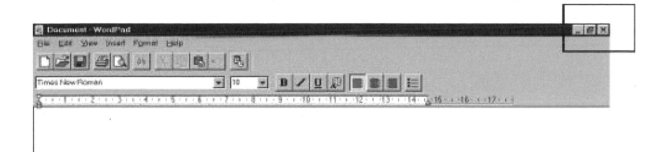

Diag 11 – Closing a program

Switching off your computer

The procedure for switching off your computer is very much the reverse of booting up. Close all the programs that are open using the method given above (diagram 10a).

□ Place the mouse pointer over the start button and click the left mouse button.

□ Place the mouse pointer over 'Shut Down' and click the left mouse button.

□ A 'Shut Down' window will appear asking you what you want the computer to do.

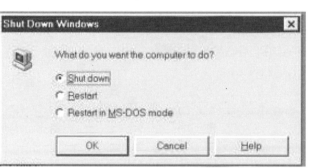

Diag 12 – The Shut Down menu

□ Place the mouse pointer over the words 'Shut Down' and click the left mouse button.

□ Place the mouse pointer over 'OK' and click the left mouse button.

□ After a few moments the computer will power down and the message 'IT IS NOW SAFE TO TURN OFF YOUR COMPUTER' will appear on the screen.

□ You may now turn off your computer.

Wordprocessing programs for professionals

Now that you have created a document in Wordpad you can really appreciate the marvels of wordprocessing software. By using Wordpad you have prepared yourself for the more up-market wordprocessing programs and will be able to appreciate the extra facilities that they offer.

One such wordprocessor is *Corel® WordPerfect® 8 for Linux®* – the Personal Edition lets you manage over 40 different file formats, including Microsoft® Word 2002 files. Instead of going to the menu bar you can change margins and columns directly on your page. Whilst typing, the program identifies grammatical phrases and provides alternative words that may be more suitable. Spelling errors are a thing of the past: the Spell-As-You-Go™ feature is turned on automatically when you start the program. Misspelt or mistyped words are underlined with red. To correct misspelt words, clicking the right mouse button once on the misspelt word opens a window from which you can select the correct spelling.

If you have images in your document you have the option of moving, rotating and sizing an image within a box. Text can be wrapped on both sides of an image, or you can even contour text around odd shapes. You can also draw objects directly on top of text, group graphics and add colour gradient fills or patterns.

Microsoft® Word 2002 is another excellent professional wordprocessor that is full of essential utilities similar to Corel® WordPerfect® 8. Most of the tools and commands you need are easy to find on the Standard and Formatting toolbars and on the Word menus. If you need help, type your question in the 'Office Assistant' that sits in the corner of the screen, and then click the left mouse button on 'Search'. Most often your query will be dealt with quickly and efficiently.

The 'Spell checker' and 'Grammar checker' is a great help, saving much time on proofreading when typing long documents. There is a similar feature to Spell-As-You-Go™ in Corel® WordPerfect® 8. Misspelt words are automatically underlined with corrections being made whilst typing.

Long documents can also be proofread using the 'Spellcheck' facility. You will find similar spellcheckers in most good wordprocessing programs. The following method is a feature of Microsoft® Word 2002.

With the left mouse button Select 'Tools' on the menu bar. On the drop down menu that appears select 'Spelling and Grammar'. The 'Spelling and Grammar' window will open. Words not in the program dictionary will be highlighted in a window with alternative suggestions beneath. You will be given the opportunity to ignore the suggested word(s), add them to the dictionary or change the spelling. When all the document has been spell checked the window will close. Microsoft® Word 2002 also gives you the opportunity to check the grammatical sense of your document in a similar way to spell checking.

Universal shortcuts whilst working with programs

Most wordprocessor programs provide keyboard shortcuts for manipulating text without taking your hands off the keyboard. Some people, especially 'touch typists' find that this feature saves time and effort when inputting data and typing documents. The list is by no means complete. Each program that you use will have variations from the norm. The following list of shortcuts are used in most popular wordprocessing programs. For a more comprehensive list refer to the help menu in the program that you are using.

- To switch to the window you last used or switch to the next window – press **ALT** while repeatedly pressing **TAB**.

- To undo the last action you performed – press **CTRL+Z**

☐ To save your file to disk – press **CTRL+S**

☐ To copy selected text or data – press **CTRL+C**

☐ To paste text or data from the pasteboard – press **CTRL V**

☐ To bold selected text – press **CTRL+SHIFT+B**

☐ To cut selected text or data – press **CTRL+X**

☐ To quit a program – press **ALT+F4 (Make sure you have saved your work before committing this action)**

☐ To select all the text in a document – press **CTRL+A**

☐ To delete a word – press **CTRL+BACKSPACE CTRL+DELETE**

☐ To delete to the end of a line – press **SHIFT+END, DELETE**

☐ To delete to the end of a page – press **SHIFT+DOWN ARROW** (to end of page), **DELETE**

☐ To delete to the left word boundary – press **CTRL+BACKSPACE**

SPREADSHEETS

The basic use of spreadsheets is to manipulate data in the form of calculations. It is an ideal environment for keeping records, graphical displays and charts of all kinds. Because of the complexities of mathematical formulae, it is not possible to teach the novice how to use spreadsheets to their full capacity. Spreadsheet software is not provided with Microsoft Windows, but there are many third party programs available. Microsoft Office® provides Microsoft Excel®, which is one of the leading programs and is used in the following examples. There are many other programs such as: Foxpro®, Corel® WordPerfect® 8 for Linux® and Microsoft® Works for Windows®.

When you create a spreadsheet the window displays a worksheet with a grid of rows and columns. Each cell has a reference indicating its row and column location, for example, 'A1'. The standard 'Menu bar' is displayed at the top of the screen in the same way as you have already seen in your wordprocessor. Icons displayed underneath the 'Menu bar' are for formatting, to provide easy access to common tasks.

☐ On the File menu, left mouse click '**New**'. A new spreadsheet will be displayed.

☐ Click the left mouse button in cell 'A1', enter 123.

☐ Click the left mouse button in cell 'B1', enter 25.

□ Click the left mouse button in cell 'C1', enter =A1*B1.

□ The answer 3075 will display in cell 'C1'.

□ Similarly if you enter 19 in cell 'A2'.

□ 109 in cell 'B2'.

□ and =A2*B2 in cell 'C2'.

□ You will get the answer 2071.

	A	B	C	D
1	123	25	3075	
2	19	109	2071	

Diag 13 – Cells in a spreadsheet

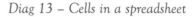

Diag 14 – A Spreadsheet

Moving or copying cells

When you move or copy a cell, the information within the cell doesn't change. To move the cell, drag the selection with the left mouse button depressed to the upper-left cell of the paste area. Any information already in that paste area will be lost as your program will replace any existing data with the new data that you have pasted or copied.

To copy a cell – place the mouse pointer over the cell, hold down the left mouse button plus 'Control'. Then drag the cell to the new location.

Moving blocks of cells – To move a block of cells, click the left mouse button on the first cell of the range, then keeping the left mouse button depressed drag the mouse pointer to the last cell. Click the left mouse button on the corner of the selected block of cells and then keeping the left mouse button depressed, drag the cells to the new location.

Data alignment – To align data at the top, centre, or bottom of a cell, click the left mouse button on the cells you want to format. On the 'Format' menu, click with the left mouse button on 'Cells', and then click the left mouse button on the 'Alignment' tab. Select the option you want in the 'Vertical' box.

Microsoft Excel Office Assistant – Office Assistant is available any time by pressing 'F1' on the keyboard. It can answer your questions, offer tips, and provide Help for a variety of features specific to the program you are in. The Assistant can display any of the following:

Tips – Point out how to use the features or keyboard shortcuts in the program more effectively. A tip is available when a yellow light bulb appears in the Assistant; click with the left mouse button on the light bulb to see the tip. If the Assistant is not visible when a tip arrives, the Office Assistant button displays a light bulb. Click Office Assistant to display the Assistant, and then click the light bulb to display the tip.

Check spelling or automatically correct spelling errors – You can check spelling on all types of spreadsheets. If you use words that aren't in the main dictionary then you can add words to a custom dictionary. Microsoft Excel will then question the words only if they're misspelt.

The AutoCorrect feature – In Microsoft Excel you can correct many common typing errors as you work; for example, it can change 'teh' to 'the' and change 'havent' to 'haven't'. The 'AutoCorrect' feature can be found on the 'Tools' menu where you can add new AutoCorrect entries to correct additional words you often mistype.

Many of the features shown are available in other third party spreadsheets but work in different formats. Look in the help files of the program that you are using to get the best results for your work.

Ready-to-use forms and templates

Spreadsheet forms is the one solution to all your form creation needs. Whether you create a form from scratch or use a pre-designed form, forms will do the job and do it easily! Most spreadsheet programs automate the common tasks of filling in invoices, expense statements, and purchase orders. Usually templates for these forms are available within the program when purchased. To use the templates, click New on the File menu, and then double-click a template on the menu window. The opening screen is your door to the easiest way to create forms. The program will assist you in your task of designing a form. You can create a form, modify an existing form or fill a pre-selected form with data.

Since every custom form is unique, there is no set procedure that you can follow. Your spreadsheet program will have many features that will enhance the form you are creating and adding and filling those fields, adding graphic images, having enhanced drawing tools such as rounded box or freehand lines, easily creating tables.

You can create your own forms by setting up a worksheet with the text, graphics and formatting you want and then saving the spreadsheet as a template. To fill out a blank copy of the form, use as a base a new form on the template by using the **'New'** command on the **'File'** menu. Users can also print the form and fill out the form on paper. After you finish creating a form, turn off the display of cell gridlines before you save the form.

☐ Click the left mouse button on **'Options'** on the **'Tools'** menu.

☐ Click the left mouse button on the **'View'** tab, and then clear the Gridlines check box. You can include on a form drawing objects that you create with the **'Drawing'** toolbar.

Saving a spreadsheet

When you save a file for the first time, you assign a file name and indicate where you want to store the file on your computer's hard disk or in another location. Each time you subsequently save the file, your spreadsheet is updated with your latest changes.

☐ Left mouse button click on **'File'**.

☐ Using the left mouse button click on **'Save'** on the drop down menu.

☐ In the **'Save File'** window, Click the left mouse button on the drive or folder where you want to save the file.

☐ Enter the file name in the box provided, then use the left mouse button to click on **'OK'**.

Opening a spreadsheet that has been saved

☐ Use the left mouse button to click on **'File'**, then left mouse button click on **'Open'** on the drop down menu.

☐ In the **'Open File'** window, use the left mouse button to click on the drive or folder that contains the file you want to open.

☐ In the folder list, use the left mouse button to double-click on folders until you open the folder that contains the file you want.

Deleting a spreadsheet

☐ Using the left mouse button, click on **'File'**, then left mouse button click on **'Open'**.

□ In the 'Open File' window, click the drive or folder that contains the file you want to delete.

□ In the folder list, double-click folders until you open the folder that contains the file you want.

□ Using the right mouse button click on the file you want to delete, and then click 'Delete' on the shortcut menu.

Printing the spreadsheet

□ Use the left mouse button to click on the 'File menu'.

□ Select 'Print' using the left mouse button.

□ In the 'Print window', use the left mouse button to click on 'OK'.

Closing the spreadsheet

□ Use the left mouse button to click on the 'File menu'.

□ Select 'Close' using the left mouse button.

□ If you have made alterations since you last saved your spreadsheet the program will ask you if you want to save your file. A window will be displayed showing three options: 'YES – NO – CANCEL'. Use the left mouse button to click on 'YES'.

When you have finished working in your program:

□ Use the left mouse button to click on 'File'

□ Use the left mouse button to click on 'Exit' on the drop down menu.

□ Your program will now automatically close down and your desktop will be displayed.

DESKTOP PUBLISHING

Desktop publishing software lets you integrate text and images imported from a wide variety of sources. In particular, you should note that it can be done using separate applications (such as your wordprocessor for text, or paint program for graphics).

Text

Text can be typed directly onto the page. Use the 'Text' tool to type the text directly into the page area. This is the ideal way to create headlines, captions and other small amounts of text used as part of your design.

Alternatively, you can create text using your existing wordprocessing programs, such as Windows WordPad and then save it as a separate file. It can then be then be imported into your DTP.

Once you have decided on your design, and you know what text and graphics you want to use, you're ready to start the actual page make-up stage.

- □ Start with a new, blank page.

- □ Click the left mouse button on **'File'** then on **'New'**, then choose a page size.

You can change this page size later, and modify the margins if necessary, using **'Page'** or **'Page Setup'**. All subsequent page layout work will build on this page setup.

The layout

Once a basic publication setup is defined you are ready to create a layout or layout grid consisting of columns, guides and text frames. The grid is very important as it defines how your page will look and ensures page to page consistency.

Adding headlines

Now add major text elements like headlines and captions using the **'text'** tool to create free text blocks. Apply text formatting commands using the **'Text'** menu to get the text looking the way you want it. Adjust the font, size, width, and colour. Rotate the text for greater impact.

You can use your desktop printer to produce up to A4-size prints. A printer that prints up to A3 size is even better if you want to print large size posters, calendars and so on.

Save your work

Finally, save your file by clicking the left mouse button on **'File'** then **'Save'**.

Wizards

Most of the work done in desktop publishing programs (DTP) is carried out by the automated 'wizards', which will help you to start your 'Home Publishing' business right away! You will be able to create a finished publication that you can be proud to exhibit. Most, if not all DTPs will help you to create 'Newsletters', 'Business Cards', 'Letterheads', 'Forms', 'Sales material', 'Greetings cards' and a host of other office and home material.

- □ To view the projects wizard place the mouse pointer over the chosen icon.

- □ Press the left mouse button once.

- □ Place the mouse pointer over **'Next'**.

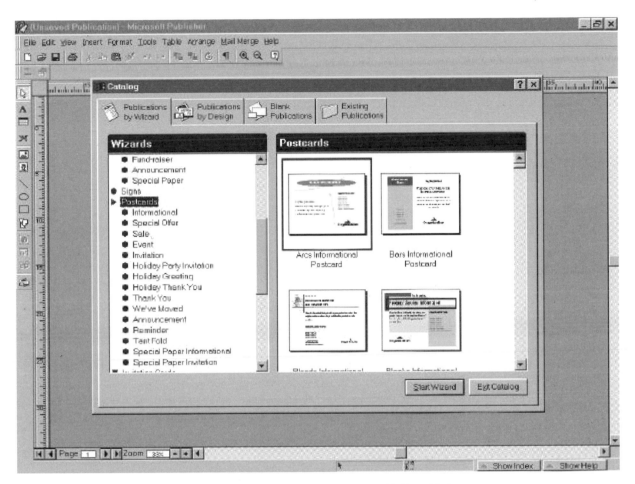

Diag 15 – Opening Wizards Display of MS Publisher

□ The wizard will now take you to another display with more wizards. Choose the required wizard in the same way as before.

□ The wizard will now ask you a series of questions so that it can build a picture ready for printing. Press **'Next'** to begin.

□ Enter the relevant details in the window where the cursor is blinking. Press **'Next'**. You will be asked to repeat this action until all relevant information has been entered.

□ Finally, press **'Finished'**.

The completed document will now be displayed.

Print the document in the same way as previously shown in your **'Wordpad'** program.

You can use desktop publishing software to place text and graphics without constraint anywhere on the page. Desktop publishing software is not suitable to create detailed graphics. This is probably because desktop publishing can become quite difficult. Since creating graphics can also be complicated, you are likely to use a different application for each task. This usually works out, since most desktop publishing programs are very good about accepting the graphics you create in most computer graphics programs.

Typical pages from two leading desktop publishing programs are shown below:

Diag 16 – A Trifold Leaflet

Diag 17 – A Newsletter

The toolbar

The 'Toolbar' (see Diag 18) contains tools for selecting, altering text that you have already typed (editing) and creating frames for placing text on any part of the page (text frames). Frames can also be placed containing graphics and pictures.

The 'Pointer' tool lets you select, move, resize, copy or edit text and objects. All you have to do is left mouse click on the pointer, move the pointer over the text or object to be altered and click the left mouse button.

The 'Rotate' and 'Crop' tools let you select an object then rotate or crop (trim or resize) the selection.

When the 'Text' tool is selected, (that's the tool with the letter 'A') you can place text in a frame on the page. You can create headlines and captions by clicking over a blank area of the page then typing. To move the text, select the 'Pointer' tool then left mouse button click on the text. By keeping the left mouse button depressed drag the pointer and text to the part of the page where you want the text to be placed.

Zoom In	F6
Zoom Out	Shift+F6
Paste	Ctrl+V
Insert	▶
Select All	Ctrl+A, F2
Grid Options...	
✔ Snap to Grid	Ctrl+G
Page Setup...	
Layer Manager...	
Default Properties...	

Diag 19 – Shortcut Dropdown menu

The 'Picture' tool button is depicted on the tool bar by an icon, usually a 'head' or 'panoramic view'. When you left mouse button click on the 'Picture' tool a window will open for you to choose the graphic or picture that you want to import into your page. If the picture is too big or too small use the 'Crop' tool to resize the picture.

The 'Drawing' tools are for creating lines, boxes and ovals. When the tool is selected depress the left mouse button and drag the pointer across the page to create a line or shape. Release the mouse button when the line or shape has been created to the size that you require.

Diag 18
The Toolbar

Shortcuts

When you have selected an area of 'Text' or a 'Picture' you can use the right mouse button to see a drop down menu similar to the one shown in Diag 19.

COMPUTER GAMES

Microsoft© has included several computer generated games in Windows that can be located from your desktop.

With the left mouse button select 'Start', 'Programs', 'Accessories', 'Games'. Then select the game of your choice.

The four games included with your software are:

Freecell – This is a card game. To win, you have to make four stacks of cards on the home cells: one for each suit, stacked in order of rank.

Hearts – This is another card game. The object of Hearts is to have the lowest score at the end of the game.

Minesweeper – Starting with a playing field divided into blank squares the object is to find all the mines on the playing field as quickly as possible without uncovering any of them.

Solitaire – This game is played in the same way as the ordinary card game (sometimes called Patience).

USING 'PAINT'

Windows includes a program called 'Paint' in which you can create, view and edit graphics. It will accept most types of graphic files for you to view and then paste into other programs.

To draw your own pictures do the following:

After choosing one of the drawing tools in the 'Toolbar' use the left mouse button to draw circles, lines, squares or oblongs. Other tools allow you to draw freehand.

To paint an area or object with colour click the required tool in the tool box with the left mouse button, and then click a colour from the colour box. Then click and hold down the left mouse button in the area or object you want to paint.

Saving Files – The method of saving a file in 'Paint' is exactly the same as you have previously been shown in 'Wordpad'. Go to 'File' on the menu bar. Select 'Save' on the drop down menu and enter a name for your file.

Chapter 9

Earning Money With Your Computer

The invention of the home computer has created many opportunities to run a home-based business thus enabling a vast number of people to earn money from home. Any computer suitable for home use will get you started. Large volumes of information can be stored on the hard disk, zip drive or on rewriteable CDs. Today's printers will give you superior printing, matching professional standards.

Desktop publishing

Desktop publishing packages are available on CD for most computers. This will complement most word processors and add artwork to your designs. Sometimes they come as a complete package with your computer system. They will allow you to produce quality printing and artwork, which will help you save money by typesetting advertisements yourself.

A fax and telephone are essential. If you have a telephone line then it is simplicity in itself to set up your computer to send and receive faxes and take messages for you. You will also be able to print your own business stationery such as letterheads, compliments slips and business cards.

One of the most productive areas of home based businesses is with accounts. There are many accounts packages available to enable anyone with a little knowledge of accounting to create a lucrative business run from home.

Astrology

The astrological columns in newspapers and magazines today are generally based on the signs of the zodiac and the location of the Sun when a person was born. This is a simplified form of astrology, which implies that all people born under the same sign anywhere in the world at any time share common characteristics and that their daily activities should be so guided. Astrological programs predicting horoscopes are widely available for use on your computer. This gives a more individual analysis when casting a horoscope for clients by noting the relationships of the Sun, Moon, planets, and signs of the zodiac to the time and place of their birth.

Astrology is big business in all parts of the world, where countless clients want to have their horoscope read. Not everybody wants to do the research themselves: research is time-consuming and not everyone enjoys it. This is a very good business opportunity for anyone keen on astrology and who can operate a home computer.

Some packages allow you to tap into a vast reserve of astrological information particularly from the Internet. Data and details relating to star signs, and much more, will be of interest to thousands of customers.

Potential earnings vary from moderate to potentially very high indeed. Some similar businesses extend their services over a wide area, using the Internet to reach customers all over the world.

Accounts

There are many accounting packages on the market with little to choose between any of them. Flexibility of use has always been the main focal point of every production of accounts software.

Most accounts programs allow you to get all the information you want quickly and easily by looking at only one screen. This screen is your own custom-made profile of the financial presentation, so you see only what you want to see, with relevant up-to date information which lets you understand the complete financial situation at a single glance.

Diag 20 – Accounts Bankstatement

Accounts packages are designed to look and work exactly like a bank statement – there is nothing new to learn. They use no accounting jargon or complex instructions.

You can start working with accounts with very little to understand, by simply inputting a few numbers from your client's latest bank statement.

CV and résumé service

Writing opportunities are plentiful, particularly for specialist writers who can offer a service to write CVs and résumés. In addition, if you can write and can provide pictures to accompany your work you could well be employed in a full-time and profitable business.

A wordprocessing program is now an essential piece of equipment for the writer, who can change, amend and rewrite articles. Your main client base will include students, training establishments, correspondence colleges, and so on. Market your business in college magazines designed for your target clientele.

Use your computer as a phone/answer phone business

Provided your computer has a modem and the correct hardware and software, you will be able to use your computer to dial out; just like you would when you use your telephone. For home and small business use, BT's 'Home Highway' installation kit is a worthwhile installation to get the best out of your equipment.

The demand for telephone answering services continues to grow. Today's successful business person wants the personal touch of a friendly, professional assistant answering their phones for them. The professional answering service operator can pass information along the proper channels to the different callers, take messages, get clarifications and even set up meetings with special customers. In many instances, businessmen come to think of the operators at their telephone answering service as vital to their success.

Using your computer as a fax machine

There are many software programs designed to send faxes from which to choose. The best program for you depends on the number and type of documents you want to fax. Your fax can consist of a fax cover page accompanied by your letter, report, and/or a spreadsheet. The most popular fax programs can be accessed by clicking on 'Print' in the 'File Menu' on your wordprocessor or spreadsheet program. Change the choice of 'printer' in the print window to 'Fax' and then follow the instructions given by the fax program.

With automatic reception enabled, you will be able to receive incoming messages automatically as long as the fax program is running. To enable the fax program to be running whenever your computer is turned on, place a shortcut to the program in the start-up folder as follows:

With the left mouse button click the 'Start button' and then move the mouse pointer to 'Settings'.

Click the left mouse button on 'Taskbar & Start Menu', then click the left mouse button on the 'Start Menu Programs' tab.

Click the left mouse button on 'Add' and click again on 'Browse'.

In the 'Browse' window locate your fax program folder, open it by using the left mouse button to double-click on its folder, then find the fax program icon and click on it with the left mouse button.

Click the left mouse button on 'Open' and then double-click the left mouse button on the 'StartUp folder'.

Type the name that you want to see on the 'StartUp' menu, and then click the left mouse button on 'Finish'. On some desktops the Windows program prompts you to choose an icon suitable for the program, click the left mouse button on your chosen icon and then click the left mouse button on 'Finish'.

Next time you start your computer the fax program will be running in the background. When a fax is received the program will alert you to its progress.

In summary

It is now accepted worldwide that computers are an essential part of any business. Letters, memos and reports are just a few of the many different documents created on a computer transforming plain documents into effective, professional communications. The speed and efficiency of modern equipment ensures that accurate records can be maintained and stored and then retrieved at the touch of a button. With the attachment of peripherals, such as the modem, up to the minute information can be transmitted and received, saving on time and cost. Also, constant contact with personnel can be maintained wherever they may be.

Any business, whether it is a large corporation or one person working from home, can in effect become part of a network of successful businesses, with the advantages of using a computer to take part in video-conferencing with business associates anywhere in the world.

Part Three
The Internet – Surfing The Net

Chapter 10

Surfing the Net

The Internet is a network of computers that connects millions of computers around the world. A program such as 'Microsoft Internet Explorer' enables you to join this network to gain access to the immense stores of information on these computers.

Although it is not, strictly speaking, a computer peripheral, the Internet is becoming so important in the world of computing that it deserves to be considered as a potential part of any computer system. Certainly, it allows almost unrestricted access to a huge variety of information, software and leisure areas, and provides the facility to communicate quickly and easily with people all around the globe. As ever-increasing numbers of people and companies get connections, its importance as a means of making contact with people will grow. The Internet is no more a trendy fad than fax machines have proven to be; in a short space of time, access to it will be considered an indispensable part of the business furniture.

In the beginning

The Internet started life in American research labs. In the early 1980s, it was decided that a flexible means of communication was necessary, one that could, in theory, survive a serious catastrophe or a dedicated attack, such as a limited nuclear strike. Unlike conventional systems such as the telephone, which rely on having signals connected from one end to another, the new network would bounce its messages from place to place indirectly. If one part of the network was removed, the information would simply flow around the gap. By connecting computers into a big, sprawling mass rather than in straight lines, any part of the group could get a message through to any other part of the group without having to take any route in particular. If the centre was destroyed, the edges could still pass information around each other. The research was extremely successful, and university computers were allowed to join the military ones in order to help the network grow and establish itself. After all, the more computers that were connected, the stronger the communication links would be. Rather than rely on public telephone networks, permanently connected fixed lines were installed all across the network. In some cases, radio and satellite data relays were also put in place in case major cabling became badly disrupted. The Internet was born.

Into the future

Some fifteen years later, the original vision, whilst being completely fulfilled, has also been rather swamped. Word spread from the universities and other countries set up similar systems. As the students and professors moved into the business world, they carried the word of this system with them, and it moved beyond the research world and into the public domain.

It was not until it became possible to organise text and images into easily-accessed magazine-style information pages (the *World-Wide Web* or *WWW* mentioned earlier) that public interest was really caught up and the connection explosion truly started. Current estimates are that there are now some 50 million people with Internet access, and the rate of connection is increasing, not decreasing. Within a few years, the Internet will be as common as the telephone and television.

Get connected

Getting a connection to the Internet is quite simple. As well as a computer, you need to have a modem so that your machine can talk down telephone lines. Once that is in place, you need to chose an *Internet Service Provider (ISP)* and ask them to send you a disk with their software, so that you can load it onto your computer. This software allows you to set up an account on-line with the ISP, then you are free to start surfing the Internet. There are many ISP companies that will provide this service for you and their numbers are growing all the time. The Internet itself is just a large group of computers that pass information to each other. There is no centre to it; it was designed not to have one. Any computer that is connected to the Internet becomes part of it. When you purchase an Internet account, you purchase the right to connect your computer to someone else's and to have that other machine pass Internet information down to you.

Internet Service Providers

Connection to the Internet is provided by companies known as *Internet Service Providers* (or ISPs); when you dial into their machine, they connect you straight through to the Internet, so that your machine becomes part of the network. While you are connected, you are actually part of the information transfer system. All of your messages and Internet-related programs are stored on your machine, and you can do anything that you wish to and that you have the correct software to do. Messages come through to you directly and are stored on your machine, although they are held waiting for you when your machine is not hooked up (the term most commonly used is *logged on*).

There are two ways that you can be charged for your access to the Internet – most ISPs offer you a choice of ways. For those that do not anticipate using the Internet a great deal, the cheapest way is usually to subscribe to a service where you pay a local call rate for the time that you are logged on. The alternative type of subscription is where you pay a standard monthly fee for the access, and you are given a freephone number so that there are no call charges. Currently the cost of the flat fee is around £15 per month, but this varies from ISP to ISP, so make sure that you understand what you will be paying for before you sign up to a service.

For beginners, the best way to chose an ISP is to ask any of your friends which company they use as their ISP. Each ISP varies – some may be relatively cheap but have a problem with too many subscribers, meaning that it is difficult to get a connection; others may be simple to set up on your machine; some may offer other benefits to small businesses but be relatively expensive for personal use.

File Transfer Protocols

Two other Internet tools are slightly different. FTP is the name given to the service that allows you to connect to another machine on the Internet and copy information from it to your own computer. Not all Internet computers are open for FTP connection – you have to set it up specially – but those that are hold software, information, pictures and just about anything else that can be stored and transmitted via computer. The complementary service to FTP is called Telnet. Rather than allowing you to connect and copy files, this lets you connect to another computer as if you were actually sitting in front of it. Again, most computers are not available for public Telnet access, but some are; these usually host discussion areas, live chat sessions or actual accounts on a large mainframe computer.

Take an overview

When you are looking at Internet accounts, you want to be sure that you are able to get unrestricted access to all of these facilities: email, WWW, IRC, Usenet News, FTP and Telnet are all extremely useful. There are other, less important Internet tools that also may or may not be available, but they are far less significant. In particular, some companies choose to censor the list of Usenet News groups that they will let you access, so you may wish to make enquiries about that. You should also check that the company provides a local-call access number for your area, so as to save you from grotesque telephone bills, and that they have a maximum modem speed that is at least as high as your modem's maximum speed. Other things to consider include the number of connections that they can accept at any one time, for some of the smaller companies may have significantly more members than they do phone lines. This can mean hours of endless frustration as you attempt to get an answer from the company rather than an engaged signal. You are not necessarily better off with a big company; some of the smaller ones are able to give a far more effective and personal connection. As with all cases where you are purchasing a service, friendly recommendations are often a good guide.

There can be no doubt that as time goes by the importance of the Internet can only grow and grow. It is already too useful and profitable to fizzle away. Even if you do not have much personal interest, you should be aware that in the years to come it will probably be more of an accepted part of everyday life. That alone makes it worth taking into account when you are buying a computer system. Once you start to explore the Internet, you will come across all sorts of weird and wonderful sites. You will be able to take part in 'Chat Rooms' where you will be able to talk to like-minded people. Information that you once thought was unavailable will be right at your fingertips. You can get the latest news from newspapers before it reaches the newstand. Link up with relatives and friends; send them letters and pictures all for the cost of a local telephone call and in some instances free of charge.

When you subscribe to your favourite sites (web sites) you can have the content automatically updated

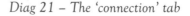

Diag 21 – The 'connection' tab

whenever you want – daily, weekly, or monthly. Internet Explorer can download updated Web pages or entire sites in the background while you do other work on your computer, or even while you sleep. Then you can look at them later online, offline, at work, at home, or while travelling.

Once you have registered with a 'Server' all you have to do is click the left mouse button on the 'Connection' tab, and then follow the instructions on your screen.

You can search for web sites using the Explorer bar. Click the 'Search' button on the toolbar: the Explorer bar appears in the left side of the browser window. Then you can use the left mouse button to click on a link to view that page on the right side of your screen while still viewing the list of search results on the left. You can similarly browse through your Favourites and History folders, channels, or your documents. With an Internet connection and Microsoft Internet Explorer, you can find and view information on just about anything on the Internet.

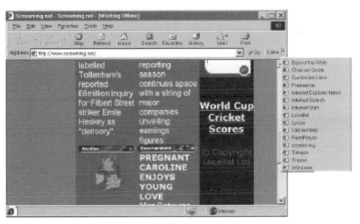

Diag 22 – Windows Explorer Links sub-menu

Create a button on the 'Links' toolbar just by dragging a link to it from the 'Address' bar or a Web page. You can easily customise the 'Links' toolbar to display buttons the way you want them. Alternatively, add a Web page to your list of favourites for easy access from the 'Favourites' menu or Explorer bar.

Searching the web

You can find information on the Web in a variety of ways. When you click the 'Search' button on the toolbar, the Explorer bar appears at the left of the window. It provides access to a number of search services that offer different kinds of searching capabilities. Try out the different search services to see what kinds of information they provide.

If you want to find information extra quickly, you can use the 'AutoSearch' feature by typing 'Go', 'Find', or '?' followed by a word or phrase, right in the Address bar. Internet Explorer immediately starts a search using its predetermined search service.

Then, after you go to a Web page, you can search for specific text on that page.

Diag 23 – The Menu bar

To enter a web address

In the Address bar, type the Web address you want to go to.

If you have visited the web site before, the AutoComplete feature suggests a match as you type. The suggested match is highlighted in the Address bar.

After you finish typing the Web address, or when AutoComplete finds a match, click the left mouse button on **'Go'**.

To view other matches, press the **'DOWN ARROW'** key on your keyboard.

After you go to a Web page, you can search for specific text on that page.

To revisit recently viewed web pages

On the toolbar, click the left mouse button on the **'History'** button.

A list of folders appears, containing links for web sites visited in previous days and weeks.

Click the left mouse button on a folder or page to display the Web page.

Offline browsing

With offline browsing, you can view Web pages without being connected to the Internet. You can browse by using channels and subscriptions to get the latest content downloaded to your computer when you are connected and online. Then view the Web pages offline when you want, where you want.

Printing a web page

When you print a Web page, you can print the page as you see it on the screen, or you can print selected parts of it, such as a frame. In addition, you can specify that you want to print additional information in the headers and footers, such as the window title, page address, date, time, and page numbers.

To print the contents of the current window

On the **'File'** menu, click the left mouse button on **'Print'**.

Sending and receiving email

With 'Outlook Express' you can exchange email with friends or join 'chatgroups' to exchange views and information. To read your messages, click the left mouse button on the 'Send/Recv button on the toolbar; you can then read messages either in a separate window or in the preview pane or when you click with the left mouse button on the **'Inbox'** icon on the **'Outlook'** bar or the folders list.

To view the message in the preview pane, double click the left mouse button on the message in the message list.

To save a message in a designated file folder, click the left mouse button on '**Save as**' and then select the location for the file to be saved.

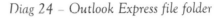

Diag 24 – Outlook Express file folder

Address books

The address book provides a convenient place to store contact information for easy retrieval by most programs. It also features access to the Internet directory services that you can use to look up people and businesses on the Internet.

To open the address book from 'Outlook Express', click the '**Addresses**' button on the toolbar, or click the '**Tools**' menu and Select '**Address book**'.

You can store names and addresses in your Address Book automatically by simply replying to a message or by importing them from other programs. Other methods include typing them in or by adding them from email messages that you receive.

Diag 25 – The Address Book window

Attaching files to email messages

To insert a file in a message, click the left mouse button anywhere in the message window. On the Insert menu, left mouse click '**File Attachment**' and then locate the file you want to attach. Select the file and then click the left mouse button on '**Attach**'. You will see the file named in the '**Attach**' box in the message header.

Diag 26 – Attaching a file to an email

Internet servers

There are many other programs giving access to the Internet. America On Line, AOL, is a particularly good server making it very easy to get on line. The email facility is second to none. Easy to use 'help' instructions guide you through every aspect of 'surfing the net'. There is also free online help and free telephone contact if you get into difficulties. Other servers include 'Screaming Net' which, incidentally, gives free telephone connection as well as free online time, 'One-to-One', and 'Freeserve'. All give a good service.

Free software on the net

The Internet is more than just a place to download the latest game demos, shareware, freeware and other computer-related files from libraries. There are also free music web-sites as well. If you check out the main Web directories, you will find what is available.

If you want to make your own web page, you will find what is on offer regarding free web space at 'http://www.freewebspace.net'.

Free email services are indexed at the 'Free Email Providers Guide': 'http://www.fepg.net'.

If you are interested in games there is one address you should visit: 'http://www.gamersinn.com/library.html.' The Gamer's Inn is a growing community of gaming enthusiasts, game players and gamers who enjoy interacting with each other.

At http://www.free classical music is available. Listen to midi music on Composers.htm. You can also listen to a full library of classical music by many famous composers, such as Bach, Mendelssohn, Debussy, Haydn and many more.

Check into Free Radio to listen to music any time you have a moment to spare. Type in the address: 'http://www.Internet\Free Radio Prison City (FIXX 96) 95_9 FM.htm' and press 'Go'.

Want to read your favourite music magazine? Log onto 'http://www.nme.com'. Here you will find the UK's largest music news archive; you can read more reviews each week than at any other UK Site.

When you sign on to the Internet via your server you will find many channels available for you to chat with your friends and family. On **'AOL'** you will have direct access to these channels by setting up your **'Buddy List™'** which is provided by **'AOL'.**

Once on the net you are free to support any 'Chat' web page that you come across. One of the best sites is **'WWW.chat.yahoo.com'** which is very well supported. Private channels are useful if you wish to keep your conversation outside of the public domain. You would, however, have to ensure that your contact is online and using the same channel.

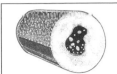
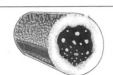

Diabetes

SPECIAL – If you have diabetes, then you need to read a remarkable new book that, according to the author, shows diabetics how to improve their blood sugar levels, boost their energy and feel 100% better – every day!

The Diabetics Guide to Healthy Living, by Maxwell Stein shows diabetics how to make lifestyle and dietary changes that will dramatically improve their health. Diabetics who have already tried the programme are raving about the results they have achieved:

Reduced Blood Sugar – Big Energy Boost!

"I have followed the programme outlined in Mr Stein's book for several weeks and I can confirm that this method really does hold the key to a healthier life for diabetics! I feel wonderful – and I have so much more energy. My blood sugar levels have fallen too!"

Caroline M, London

Neuropathy Vanishes!

"The information in your book has given me the power to transform my health and my life! I was suffering badly with neuropathy, and now my feet have completely healed! I would recommend your book to all diabetics – it's easy to understand and the programme is not complicated. I was able to make the lifestyle changes very easily – and I now enjoy much better health!"

Doreen K, Yorkshire

The Diabetics Guide to Healthy Living is the result of exhaustive scientific research. According to the author, the principles described in the book can help all diabetics and he shows how he believes you can:

- Boost your energy by eliminating ketones
- Improve blood sugar levels – bringing them down to the normal range
- Improve balance
- Enhance the body's power to heal wounds
- Improve eyesight.

Maxwell carries on to state that diabetics following the programme may notice marked improvements in other problem areas: lower blood pressure, reduced cholesterol levels, improved triglyceride levels. Common risks faced by diabetics may also be reduced.

To Order

Call our freephone orderline on **0870 225 5010** or send your payment of £9.95 plus £1.95 p&p (payable to Windsor Health) or credit/debit card details including your card number, start date, expiry date and issue number for Switch together with your name, address and book title to:

**Windsor Health,
Dept CPB2,
Emery House,
Brunel Road,
Totton,
Southampton
SO40 3SH**

Fibromyalgia Relief!

A new book reveals how to get relief from Fibromyalgia symptoms such as chronic muscle pain, fatigue, memory or concentration problems, sleeping problems, headaches, numbness and tingling, and sensitivity to cold.

The *Fibromyalgia Relief Handbook* reveals the latest information on Fibromyalgia – why its specific cause is not known, how it can best be treated and how to protect yourself from troublesome symptoms.

This book gives you specific facts on the brand new natural, alternative and medical solutions that can bring prompt and welcome relief.

You'll discover specific measures to deal with "hurting all over", tender spots, getting a good night's sleep, irritable bowel problems, and the other symptoms associated with Fibromyalgia.

The book reveals what foods help the condition, what you should know about the nutrients calcium and magnesium and what to avoid at all costs.

You'll even discover the benefits of therapeutic massage relaxation and meditation techniques, exercise – and much more.

The book gives you a full explanation of Fibromyalgia – in plain English – and why so many people suffer from it.

Many people are suffering from Fibromyalgia symptoms because they do not know where to find safe and appropriate treatment. Get all the facts.

To Order

Call our freephone orderline on **0870 225 5010** or send your payment of £9.95 plus £1.95 p&p (payable to Windsor Health) or credit/debit card details including your card number, start date, expiry date and issue number for Switch together with your name, address and book title to:

**Windsor Health,
Dept CPB2,
Emery House,
Brunel Road, Totton,
Southampton SO40 3SH**